D0902227

WHO SURVIVES?

HOW BENEFIT COSTS ARE KILLING YOUR COMPANY

WHO SURVIVES?

HOW BENEFIT COSTS ARE KILLING YOUR COMPANY

SAVING YOUR BUSINESS AND YOUR PEOPLE

WENDY LYNCH, PhD
and **HANK GARDNER, MD**

HEALTH *as* **Human Capital**™
FOUNDATION

Copyright © 2011 Wendy Lynch, PhD, Hank Gardner, MD,
Health as Human Capital Foundation

All rights reserved. No portion of this book may be reproduced or
utilized in any form, or by any electronic, mechanical, or other means
without the prior written permission of the publisher.

Printed in the United States of America, on acid-free paper.

Published by the Health as Human Capital Foundation
1800 Carey Avenue, Suite 500
Cheyenne, WY 82001
Phone: 307.433.9619
www.hhcfoundation.org

16 15 14 13 12 11   1 2 3 4 5

Lynch, Wendy D.
Who survives? : how benefit costs are killing your
company : saving your business and your people / by
Wendy D. Lynch and Harold H. Gardner.
p. cm. -- (Business series ; bk. 2)
Includes bibliographical references and index.
ISBN 978-0-9800702-1-7

1. Employee fringe benefits--United States.
2. Personnel management--United States.   I. Gardner,
Harold H. II. Title. III. Series: Business series
(Cheyenne, Wyo.) ; bk. 2.

HD4928.N6L96 2011   658.3'25
QBI10-600251

Library of Congress Control Number: 2010942318

CONTENTS

PREFACE

WHY READ THIS BOOK?
BECAUSE BENEFIT COSTS ARE KILLING YOUR BUSINESS!

Have we got your attention? We hope so. The title is not an exaggeration. If your company is like most, the burden of benefit costs is threatening its survival. Death may follow a slow, lingering process of innovation starvation when benefit costs prohibit critical investments in personnel or R&D. Or death may occur in a sudden loss of market share when expenses eventually prevent your product from being price competitive. Either way, fast or slow, companies that keep traditional benefits will die.

U.S. companies simply cannot compete locally or globally while dragging $10,000, $15,000, or $20,000 of unproductive benefits overhead per employee. The weight is too great.

So, you may ask, is this book suggesting that companies stop providing all benefits? No, this book will explain how to design them so they work for you instead of against you. Every dollar can be reallocated in ways that energize, motivate, and reward performance and success, rather than suffocating them.

Start With a Quick Check of Your Benefits Today

Answer these three true or false questions.

1. All employees have an opportunity to earn more than 10% higher income (in bonus or profit sharing) by improving their work performance. True or False

2. Your absence policies include the following: a combined set of days for paid time-off (i.e., vacation and sick time are together, with no separate sick leave) and employees receive less than 100% pay during an extended absence, such as short-term disability.[1] True or False

3. Your company provides a large portion of employees with relevant and meaningful skills training opportunities each year. True or False

The implications of your answers are large. Based on patterns we see across hundreds of companies, you can expect to see results as summarized in table 1:

Table 1: Benefits quick check answers and implications

	Answer	Implications
Question 1	TRUE	Strong performance and retention incentives
	FALSE	Up to 30% lower productivity and double turnover in top workers
Question 2	TRUE	Strong attendance incentive
	FALSE	Up to 25% higher avoidable benefit costs
Question 3	TRUE	Long-term human capital investment in performance
	FALSE	Up to 10% lower productivity

If you answered true to all three conditions, your company is already aligned to some degree. We will learn more in Chapter 3.

---

1. If you offer no paid time-off at all, you can also answer True.

If you answered false to all three conditions, you face some serious challenges:

- productivity as much as 40% below what you could be achieving, and
- benefit costs 25% higher or more than they need to be.

That's the bad news. The good news is that you can realign and change the course of your company. Just as important, realignment usually does not require new expenditures; rather, just a redistribution of expenditures you already make. With a smart reallocation of resources and well-designed policies, work, attendance, and even health will matter more to employees. Aligned policies also improve business profitability because everyone's actions are aligned with each other's.

If you believe your benefit costs are as low as possible while achieving the highest possible productivity levels, you don't need this book. If not, read on. Don't let anyone convince you that traditional benefit packages are a "cost of doing business," or the only way to attract and retain top talent. It's time to change the employment equation. Do it now. Your company's survival depends on it.

What Do We Know and How Do We Know It?

Our evidence comes from the combined learning of two careers and a large group of colleagues who have contributed to the evidence and new thinking. The two of us came from different worlds: a doctor who became an entrepreneur with a goal of improving healthcare and business outcomes; and a researcher/ statistician who started out evaluating corporate health promotion and ended up measuring the impact of economic incentives on employee performance.

Our team at Human Capital Management Services, LLC (HCMS) is trained in statistics, economics, medicine, health policy, and several other disciplines. From diverse backgrounds, we have come to the same conclusion: companies spend more on some benefits than they need to and miss opportunities to reward and retain top talent. We have strong evidence that workers are more productive, businesses are more successful, expenses are lower, and health and well-being are better when companies design their compensation and benefits in specific ways. What we have seen is that when benefits and policies are designed in ways where both parties can serve their own best interests through the same activities, such as working hard or working efficiently, results will be superior to when those policies serve the interests of one party, but not the other.

EVIDENCE: HOW WE KNOW WHAT WE KNOW (IN DETAIL)

For those interested in specifics, the evidence we use has evolved from asking a lot of questions and analyzing a lot of data. Over the past ten years, we accumulated a database that has information from many companies, including almost a million employees (as of the end of 2010, about 950,000).

We need a lot of data because individual information is not very useful for finding big patterns. We are not interested in whether a specific John Smith quit his job, missed work, or got promoted. We want to know if ten thousand John Smiths have different outcomes in a workplace that has policy A than ten thousand John Smiths in a workplace that has policy B. To do this, we look for overall patterns using statistical analysis, with the help of our talented team of researchers. We scrub large datasets, encrypt, and maintain them behind multiple firewalls according to all the strictest security rules. All individual data are masked by assigning unique, unidentifiable numbers. Essentially, the database has a million anonymous people that have no known identity; they remain hidden.

The trick to understanding how things work is by studying differences. Because our information comes from many different companies, in many different regions of the country, in different industries, with different types of workers, we are able to figure out how those differences affect business outcomes. For example:

- Is turnover different across industries? Yes
- Do healthcare costs differ by region of the country? Yes
- Do certain types of workers have more on-the-job accidents? Yes

By comparing different groups of employees and different companies, we have learned which characteristics predict which outcomes. Most patterns relating to industry, demographics, and health are commonly-known facts. They are not new discoveries. However, to learn what we learned, we added other information that few researchers have.

UNIQUE TYPES OF DATA

We know of no other database that captures the breadth of information that we have. Not only does it include information about companies, jobs, benefits, and productivity, it also includes policy information about how a company runs its business:

- What are its rules about time off?
- How does it reward good work?
- What sort of health insurance does it offer?
- Does it offer training?

Knowing the answers to these policy questions allows us to tease out how different policies influence business results, and compare whether one policy produces different results than another. This is like a mathematical whodunit. If we wonder whether absence policies have an influence on healthcare costs, we can test that theory. If we want to know if bonuses affect absenteeism, we can test that theory, too.

Using more complex statistical methods we can also use a technique that allows us to control for other factors. For example, what if we want to know if differing policies are leading employees at one company to have a higher rate of absenteeism than another company? We realize that absenteeism is related to gender, age, and job tenure. If we simply compare the two groups, one may be higher simply because the company has more women and long-tenured employees. Statistical modeling, called regression, allows us to determine not only if the absence rates of the two companies are different, but also that the difference is above and beyond what we would expect given their gender mix, average tenure, etc. We could conclude that, other things being equal, we would expect similar groups of employees to be absent more at Company A than Company B because of their differing absence policies.

Without getting technical, statistical analysis works by mathematically removing the effects of known factors such as gender, tenure, or age, and then testing what is left over. For example, we know already that younger employees have higher absence rates than older ones, women are absent more than men, and new employees are absent less than long-term employees. Thus, our statistical model will account for those effects and then determine if differences in sick-leave policy in Company A and Company B have an additional independent effect.

BUT NO TWO COMPANIES ARE THE SAME!

Sometimes people question whether the patterns we discover will apply in every case. Their argument is that just because something works in one instance, does not mean it will work in another. This is exactly why the patterns discovered here are more reliable than any corporate case study!

The approach we describe in this book was derived over a decade, across many companies, hundreds of job types, hundreds of thousands of people of all ages and education levels, and in all 50 states. What we discovered is that a combination of factors contributes to successful results. Virtually any single positive policy a company puts in place can be undermined by surrounding it with many misaligned policies. Similarly, virtually any single misaligned policy can be neutralized somewhat by surrounding it with well-designed policies.

Very few companies get all their policies "right" in ways we will call aligned. But most have some that are aligned and others that are not. If we had to study only companies that have 100% aligned policies or 100% misaligned policies, we would still be looking for examples. Instead, by examining the independent effects of each type of policy or practice within the full context of the way a company does business, we were able to identify how each contributes to business outcomes.

We also used a survey to verify what we discovered. After we identified key alignment factors, we conducted a national survey of employees to confirm that similar trends exist in workers' opinions and experiences. Over 1,800 workers took the survey and provided extensive feedback about their health, benefits use, motivation, productivity, and perceptions of their jobs (see Appendix for survey methodology).[2, 3, 4, 5] For readers who like more detail about how we drew our conclusions, you will find examples and stories in gray sections like this one throughout the book.

2. Lynch, W., Gardner, H., Melkonian, A., and Kleinman, N. Understanding Relationships Between Employee Productivity, Compensation, Job Satisfaction, and Health: Results from the Health as Human Capital Survey 2007. May, 2007; http://www.hhcfoundation. org/hhcf/Publications/Surveys/SummaryReport.pdf (accessed November 12, 2010).
3. Lynch, W., Gardner, H., Melkonian, A., and Kleinman, N.Human Capital, Motivation, and Productivity: Brief Report from the Health as Human Capital Survey 2007. May, 2007; http://www.hhcfoundation.org/hhcf/Publications/Surveys/Brief1.pdf (accessed November 12, 2010).
4. Lynch, W., Gardner, H., Melkonian, A., and Kleinman, N.Benefits, Rewards and Importance of Health: Brief Report from the Health as Human Capital Survey 2007. May, 2007; http://www.hhcfoundation.org/hhcf/Publications/Surveys/Brief2.pdf (accessed November 12, 2010).
5. Lynch, W., Gardner, H., Melkonian, A., and Kleinman, N.Worker Perceptions and Company Size: Brief Report from the Health as Human Capital Survey 2007. May, 2007; http://www.hhcfoundation.org/hhcf/Publications/Surveys/Brief3.pdf (accessed November 12, 2010).

HOW I GOT HERE

I remember the moment my career changed, when I learned my entire way of looking at the world was wrong.

No one else knew I was wrong. In fact, many people were happy to listen to my speeches, read my articles, and hire me to consult with them. They hired me because I delivered a message so many want to believe: find ways to keep employees healthy and your company will succeed. It was a non-controversial mission with an altruistic message. I enjoyed it.

So What Changed?

Three factors combined to prepare me for a drastic change in perspective.

Factor 1, Conflicting Evidence: More and more, the facts did not support my position. On too many occasions, companies invested in health promotion and still saw their costs increase significantly. In too many instances, companies experienced steep increases in the use of sick leave when there were no measurable changes in health. I witnessed two companies doing the exact same type of programs to improve health, one getting incredibly positive results, the other getting no benefit at all. Obviously, I was missing something.

To be clear, the basic premise is true: within a company, healthier people cost less and are more productive on average than their sicker colleagues. But across companies the story told by available data was not as simple:

- Trying to change the health of a workforce with wellness interventions failed more often than it succeeded.
- Even employers who had dozens of health-improvement programs still had problems with costs and absenteeism.
- No single program always improved health and no single improvement in health always decreased cost.

As a researcher, my conscience was disturbed by results this inconsistent and messy. I couldn't continue to recommend "solutions" that might or might not solve a company's problem. By continuing to advocate for 'health improvement,' was I really helping employees feel better and companies become more profitable? Or was I simply perpetuating a good story with a fairytale ending that very few achieved?

I was ready for a better answer, but had no idea where to look.

Factor 2, A New Approach: While struggling with the evidence, I began collaborating with a medical doctor/entrepreneur/business owner, my co-author, Dr. Harold "Hank" Gardner, who told me outright that my understanding of the relationship between health and business performance was incomplete.

Here was a trained physician saying that I was missing the point by focusing only on health. Unless I considered the broader incentives that drive employee behavior, I would miss fundamental opportunities to lower cost, improve productivity, and encourage workers to protect their health. Hank mentioned that most costs were related to moral hazard, an economic principle describing the tendency for consumers to use more services when someone else pays the bill, and that employers needed to spend more time focusing on wages and bonuses.

Having only a vague idea what that meant at the time, I remained frustrated. What did wages have to do with health? And how was that more important than healthcare or other issues? So, I listened, but didn't really absorb what he was saying. I applied a few of his concepts to my approach, but honestly, only the ones that didn't require rejecting fifteen years of work.

Our research projects continued, analyzing patterns of medical and absence data. I persisted in looking for health-related explanations for cost. Certainly, I insisted, the reason some employees had higher costs or used more sick leave was because they were, by definition, sicker. That was how I still looked at the world.

Again and again, our research team found inconsistent results. Why, in two different companies, did people with the same diseases have such vastly different costs and absences? And why did treatment of all diseases cost more in companies with higher health costs when the workers were not different? If it was simply differences in health that caused costs to be higher or lower, why were costs always higher in some companies? And why were some very healthy workers so unproductive?

I was ready for a new explanation, but old beliefs die hard. Several months into our collaboration, Hank and I had a conversation about patterns of costs in a company facing significant challenges. He asked what I thought about their insurance plan and absence policies. Because my answer showed I was less interested in policies and more interested in employee health, he issued me a direct challenge: make the effort to understand the over-arching influence of economic incentives or it will be difficult for you to help employers. Translation: either you consider the fundamentals of economics, or we cannot successfully work together.

For a person as far into a relatively successful career as I was, such challenges don't happen very often. I had a choice: take the challenge as an insult and continue working with my old, unsatisfactory paradigm, or accept the challenge and see if there was merit in his perspective. What did I have to lose?

I agreed to learn about Market Economics, and see where it led. If I didn't agree a year later, we would shake hands and part ways. I am so grateful I took the challenge. And we still work together eight years later.

The Most Important Economic Principle I Learned

The outcome of my new learning was a paper I wrote called "Six Principles Economists Know (and you should too)." Through the process of learning these basic principles, I gained a clear understanding of what Hank had been talking about.

Among these principles was this critical economic truth:

Your time and money matter more to you than someone else's (i.e., Moral Hazard)

I picked this one as the first principle, because of the impact it had on my thinking. It affects absolutely everything in life. Here's what I mean:

Q: *What do the following situations have in common?*

- Parents of teenagers discovering 4,500 text messages on their monthly cell phone bill
- Bank executives spending government bail-out money on bonuses or office remodeling

- Legislators adding their favorite pet project to an immensely important stimulus bill
- Homeowners finding that they can't get the prepaid contractor to finish the last part of a remodeling project

A: They are all predictable situations based on who bears the cost and who receives the benefit.

What Brought It All Together?

Factor 3, Milton Friedman's book: *Free to Choose*: It's not often that something you read changes the direction of your career, or even your perspective, but a single figure in Friedman's book[6] changed my thinking. I remember I was on a BART train, riding to a meeting in San Francisco, when I read the text explaining figure 1.

Figure 1: Four types of spending

Rather than quote his text, I will explain the figure in my own words. There are only four types of spending in the world.

---

6. Friedman M., Friedman R. *Free to Choose: A Personal Statement*. New York, Harcourt Brace Jovanovich; 1980.

Those types are determined by two conditions: whose money one is spending and on whom the money is being spent. Depending on those two conditions, spending falls into one of four boxes and each box has inherent human motivations.

Friedman pointed out that the only box with balanced motives is the one at the top left: me, spending my own money on myself. Under those conditions, I am both the person spending money on a product as well as the person who will receive the benefits of that product. So, I have dual motives to spend less (cost) and get more (benefit).

The box that grabbed my attention is in the bottom left. When I spend someone else's money, I have the tendency to spend more than if I am spending my own. Think of business dinners or company rental cars. This is the box representing classic moral hazard, where we are willing to consume more or take more risk if someone else will pay the bill or accept the consequences.

Regardless of what product or service we are talking about— including paid sick-leave and paid healthcare coverage—people consume more of it when they spend someone else's money. In other words, even healthy people will spend more when someone else pays.

So What?

Perhaps Friedman's simple categories should not have come as such a revelation, but they did. Many issues suddenly made more sense: all-inclusive versus fee-for-service healthcare; high versus low deductibles; the ineffectiveness of many government initiatives; benefit utilization patterns; employee and patient behavior; text-crazy teenagers; crooked politicians. Many of our systems are **created** to operate with either unbalanced motives or no coherent motives at all. By design they are **predetermined** to create over-consumption, uncontrolled cost or compromised quality. We built them that way!

In fact, if you hear a complaint about how people are behaving in business, society, schools, healthcare, international trade, industry, you can almost always go back and see that the problem reflects a mismatch between who the behavior is costing and who the behavior is benefiting. If benefit and cost are not both shared to some degree, we will have potentially troublesome motives. When a teenager can send text messages all she wants, but is not expected to pay for them, she will text more. If a physician's office can bring in more revenue by doing more tests, the staff will order more of them. And if the patient has insurance that will pay for the test, he is more likely to consent.

If we expand this concept about "spending" to include other types of resources such as time, effort, or property, we can suddenly explain an even broader array of frustrating problems. Each of us will use our own and others' resources in ways that maximize our own best interest. We inherently care more about protecting our own time, money, or property than someone else's.

If it is my resource, I am more likely to protect it.
If it is someone else's resource, I am less likely to protect it.

Once I grasped that ownership of the cost or benefit is such a powerful motive, it became more obvious how often we ignore its influence and hope, in vain, that other convincing strategies will work. We pay people the same amount of money to be absent as we do when they come to work and then we hope they won't use sick leave unless they're truly ill. We educate, plead, scold, promote and cajole…asking people to do what they should instead of doing what they're inclined to do because of the motives and incentives that our very system has created.

A Different Perspective

After my ongoing doubts and Hank's challenge, Friedman's figure was the final tipping point that changed the direction of my research and career forever. Economists already knew this phenomenon to be true, but I had essentially been ignorant to its underlying effects.

It explained so many of the inconsistencies that weighed on my conscience. There is no connection between health and cost, or health and absence, that exists in isolation from the context of personal ownership:

- A company that designs policies that encourage consumption of healthcare and sick leave will have higher costs and absences, independent of health or disease
- A worker who can get all healthcare and time off for no cost will care less about staying healthy than a worker who shares in some of the expense
- A company that does not reward people meaningfully for their work will not get the same level of productivity as a company that does

Finally, I could tell Hank, "I get it!"

So, Why Don't More People Get It?

I like to believe that there are millions of business leaders and human resource professionals just like me out there who just don't know about the power of economic incentives and "other people's money." These professionals probably have listened to the same arguments I did for decades: to reduce healthcare costs, you must improve health. They have not seen any evidence to the contrary.

We all operate within the realm we know. We pull the levers we have at our grasp. For me, the lever was health status. I believed: if we can simply get people healthier, costs and absence will go down. For an operations manager, the lever might be training; if we could just improve their skills, output will go up.

Admittedly, it is both frightening and humbling to admit when our view of the world is incomplete or ineffective. And, I have encountered many who would rather dismiss new thinking than face the uncomfortable reality of being wrong, or make significant changes in how they operate. But I also know that there are also many, many professionals as frustrated and doubtful as I was eight years ago. They know business could be better, employees could achieve more, operations could be more efficient, and that none of the levers they pull today are making a real difference.

Hopefully this book can provide the same challenge for many readers that I got from Hank. If you don't understand incentives, you won't be effective in achieving the business results you want. Open your mind to the possibility that forces you may not be aware of are working against you, forces you can change once you know what they are.

Accept the challenge. Grab the power of incentives. Align your workforce with company success. It's a risk worth taking.

Wendy D. Lynch, Ph.D.
Senior Scientist, Health as Human Capital Foundation

Part 1

WHAT IS KILLING
YOUR BUSINESS?

A WORK CONTRACT THAT DOESN'T WORK

CHAPTER 1

WHAT IS THE WORK CONTRACT?

Incentives: Why Does Anyone Work?

For most people, work is the required activity we exchange for income, financial stability and asset growth. But we are each motivated by and attracted to different aspects of the work experience. One may value a combination of steady pay and job security. Another may place higher value on recognition, a greater purpose, and intellectual stimulation. Some employees will be driven more by internal goals and beliefs and others by external rewards.

Anything that a worker desires or dislikes can operate as a motivating incentive at work. Positive examples include praise, money, or flexibility. Dislikes include reprimands or undesirable schedules. Clearly, not all incentives will get written into a work contract. However, what a contract *can* do is clearly define:

- what a worker needs to accomplish to earn compensation (work), and

- what forms compensation will take (pay).

The contract can align incentives such that the interests of the individual and the interests of the company are served by the same actions. That's alignment. Most important, an effective work contract avoids misaligning incentives in ways that reward workers for doing less work, the wrong activities, or doing the right work the wrong way. We will see examples of this below.

More often than not, the obvious and measureable incentives in our research have taken the form of money: wages and bonuses. That is because monetary rewards are the most tangible and deliver the clearest message about what a company values. For example, suppose I tell you your work has been exceptional, far more productive than that of any other worker, but then I award a large bonus to your colleague and none to you. At the very least you will be confused and more likely angry that I was dishonest when discussing your performance. Money matters. Pay, depending on how it is designed, can put employers and employees on the same team, or make them adversaries. It can encourage the top performers, or protect the least effective. Money talks. In cases where pay policies contradict the verbal message from business leaders, employees respond to the financial message and hear little else.

When people argue with us and say "money isn't the only thing that motivates workers," we agree completely. But ignoring its effects would also be foolish. If you get the economics *wrong*, it can undermine money's value as a powerful motivator. For example, if among a team of workers, one worker does not perform his share of work, but receives the same size bonus or raise, it can be de-motivating to the others. Similarly, if a worker receives strong praise for her performance but does not receive a bonus equivalent to that of her co-workers, it will erode her trust in communication with her superiors. Workers notice inconsistency, and equate monetary rewards with judgments about what is valued most. This can work for you or against you.

EVIDENCE: BONUS

When we measure the effects of pay and benefit policies on productivity and absenteeism, nothing has a stronger effect than performance bonuses, especially bonuses in excess of 10% of salary. We have many examples where workers who are eligible for bonuses are absent less than those who are not, as well as examples where larger bonuses were associated with a reduced likelihood of disability claims. Bonuses have a broad impact on use of all benefits and on productivity on the job, as long as they are tied to measureable outcomes on which the worker has influence.

Further evidence from our 2007 survey helped us understand bonuses even more. Controlling for other factors (age, gender, salary, and company size), respondents who were eligible for a bonus were half as likely to report they intended to quit in the next year. The size of their bonus was strongly related to how likely they were to rate their job as "great" or the "best they ever had." Bonus size and eligibility were both correlated with higher motivation.

EVIDENCE: REWARDS IN GENERAL

In the perception section of our survey, we had respondents rate their company on its reward and recognition practices by asking them to agree or disagree with statements, such as: "at my company the people who succeed are those who earned it with high performance;" "I am motivated to work hard because my effort is recognized and rewarded." As one might expect, answers to these items correlated with bonus eligibility. But, they correlated just as strongly with how much skill training was provided, whether they were given regular positive feedback, and whether they were asked to contribute ideas and make their own decisions. Bonuses are our strongest objective metric of alignment, but they seem to be associated with other work practices that reinforce worker growth and responsibility.

The Deterioration of Work Contracts

At its core, employment is the exchange of pay for work: if you do X, I will pay you Y. Unfortunately, today's work environment is not that straightforward and neither are work contracts. More often than not, people are paid for their time at work but not necessarily their output. In the past few decades, time has becomes a less and less valid measurement for work productivity. Indeed, how do we define "attendance" in a world of 24-hour connectivity and telecommuting? In reality, pay based only on time spent at work, rather than work accomplished, is a misaligned incentive. It encourages being there, rather than getting things done.

Today's employment contracts have also become more complex due to the addition of items that evolved during extreme circumstances in U.S. history, but then were never discontinued. For example, employer-based health insurance evolved during WWII as a means of 'rewarding' employees during mandatory wage freezes. During that same time, employers added paid-time-off benefits and organized labor negotiated them into permanent contracts that remain today. Pensions were in existence as far back as the late 1800s but become popular after the Depression and during WWII as well. Then, legislation during the 1970s mandated tighter regulations about employee safety with the creation of the Occupational Safety and Health Administration (OSHA) and management of pensions and benefits through the Employee Retirement Income Security Act (ERISA).

Pay In the Form of Healthcare Insurance, Sick Leave and Other Perks

The pros and cons of employer-sponsored health insurance and paid time-off are topics that go beyond the scope of what we will cover here. However, the concept of fringe benefits as a reward merits some consideration. The question is not whether people should have access to such services, but how their addition to an employment contract makes the exchange of *work* for *pay* less direct. Unlike money, which has universal value to all, some workers may value health insurance much differently than others and some might not perceive "better" insurance as a meaningful reward.

If, as a hypothetical alternative, there was an efficient and robust market from which individuals could buy health insurance directly, work contracts could include an additional payment, in the form of higher wages, to allow workers to select what they need or want. That would create a "cleaner" connection between work and pay that currently complicates the work contract with individual preferences about insurance. This is not possible in today's healthcare environment, but ideally we would advocate providing funds instead of more types of benefits whenever possible.

Instead, there is a lengthy list of expectations on the part of U.S. workers when it comes to the *pay* portion of the *pay*-for-*work* exchange. It's no longer a 'pay-for-work' world but instead an expectation of a steady income combined with paid sick-time, paid vacation-time, insurance against injury and illness, retirement account, computer equipment, phones, and life insurance. Less frequent but also offered are items such as adoption fees, child care, car allowances, tuition reimbursement, fitness facilities, and other perks.

Whether these are "good" or "bad" depends on the preferences of the individual employee. Employers should never forget that a dollar spent on any of these benefits or perks is a dollar not available for better pay or bonuses. We must always ask whether anything offered to employees is the most efficient and effective way to reward and encourage high performance.

EVIDENCE: MORE BENEFITS MAY NOT BE BETTER

The effect of benefits on workers' perception of their job is exactly opposite of the effect of bonuses. Respondents were asked whether they received various benefits from their company: health insurance, short- and long-term-disability insurance, and sick leave. Surprisingly, having more benefits was associated with a lower likelihood of rating their job as "great," and a higher likelihood of quitting soon. More alarming, having a greater number of benefits was associated with lower motivation at work.

Disappointingly, while the definition of *pay* has become more extensive and complex, measures and details about *work* have not. Workers know in great detail what they *get* but not as much what they need to *do* to earn their pay. The employment agreement seldom guides daily activity, at least in the sense of specifying clearly exactly what is expected or what will be compensated and how. All too often, the terms of a work contract are agreed upon at the start of employment and rarely seen again.

Because work is an ongoing activity, the work contract should be an active process. Today's work evaluation is like an annual medical check-up. But it should resemble an ongoing heart-rate monitor. As we will see, the more accurately and closely businesses connect *work* with *pay*, the better the chances of mutual success.

Remember, What You Pay for Is What You Attract

The design of *pay* will attract the type of worker who values that form of pay the most. If you pay large bonuses for high performance, you will attract workers who want opportunity to earn more through their efforts. If you pay low wages with generous benefits, you will attract workers who want better benefits instead of high pay. If you reward employees with a lot of paid time-off, you will attract workers who want to be at work less. Consider this as you review your overall compensation plan.

Fact: Higher Benefits Come In Exchange for Lower Wages

Compensation is finite. Workers with rich benefit packages are not getting *more* overall compensation from employers. Instead, they are getting a higher *portion* of their overall *pay* in the form of benefits instead of in the form of wages, bonus, job training, etc. Over and over, we see this trend, illustrated in figure 2 on the following page. In the past decade, employers have faced dramatic increases in benefit costs, such as health and disability insurance, and to cover those costs, wages have lagged. More often than not, wages now increase at a rate slower than inflation.

Figure 2[7] shows that employees get increasingly more pay in the form of health insurance, but they don't get more money in their

---

7. These are actual data from a large U.S. organization. Benefits trend has been "smoothed" to make the graph more readable.

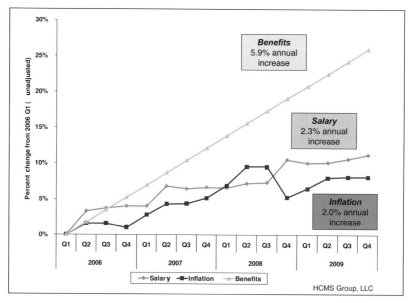

Figure 2: Benefit trend versus salary trend

pockets. This pattern is unsustainable for workers and for businesses, because it transfers resources *away* from more effective rewards that influence employee behaviors and business success. While benefits are an essential component of *pay*, above an optimal level they create misaligned incentives; that is, things get out of alignment.

If a Worker Gets Greater Value By Using Benefits... Guess What?

Viewing the benefits-wage tradeoff from the "money talks" perspective tells workers that a large part of their reward for *work* is benefits, including time off. This means workers can only get their full *pay* if they *use more absence time and benefits*. Here is an actual example of what happens as a result:

> *Workers at a large medical products company received full coverage for healthcare and full salary continuance at 100% pay during illness. The company felt these benefits were necessary to*

attract talent. We looked at a three-year period and compared medical costs and absences between month 6 and month 30 (the two years shown in the graph) for people who a) were hired in the first 6 months, b) were employed steadily for the full three years, or c) left the company in the last six months.

Figures 3 and 4 show what happened when workers planned to leave. They increased their use of all benefits to make sure they got whatever value they could. Time off increased 150% and medical costs increased 100% in the six months prior to departure,[8] even when there were no associated health complications. In order to recoup value in their employment contracts, departing workers decided to use more benefits. The company policies, paying 100% during extended absence and rich medical coverage, encouraged even higher use of extra benefits because the cost to the worker was virtually free.

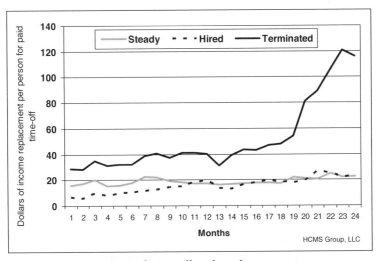

Figure 3: Paid time-off and worker transition

8. We did a specific type of regression analysis called a decomposition analysis to see if the increase in benefits use was because a) sick people, who cost more, leave the company, or b) people who leave the company cost more because they use more benefits before they leave. While both circumstances are true, we found that the pattern was much more related to the latter.

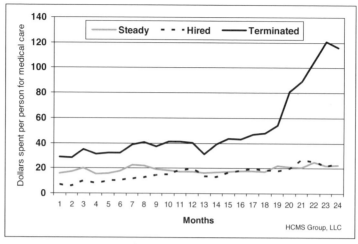

Figure 4: Medical cost and worker transition

EVIDENCE: USING BENEFITS BECAUSE YOU HAVE THEM

An interesting detail about the turnover study was that the increase in medical cost and time off occurred at every level of illness. We wanted to make sure that the effect was not simply due to a few employees getting very sick and having to quit as a result. We divided the group into low-cost employees, moderate-cost employees, and high-cost employees. In every group, those who left their jobs spent proportionately more than others in the group.

The study was the only analysis we have ever seen that confirmed a widely-suspected phenomenon: use of benefits before a work transition or policy change. We have documented this many times, showing spikes in healthcare utilization before an office closure or down-sizing, or just before an increase in health-plan deductible. The effect is predictable and measureable, especially when the worker has nothing to lose financially, such as a co-payment or a bonus as a result of being absent.

The increase in benefit use happens in varying degrees, and across any type of benefit that a worker is at risk of losing. If your company offers a Health Reimbursement Arrangement (HRA), which is a type of healthcare account whose contents are forfeited when the employee quits, you will see a spike in spending in the quarter before a worker leaves. If your company has a use-it-or-lose it policy on sick leave or vacation time, you will see a spike in absence before the days expire. In one organization that implemented a new long-term absence policy, phasing out a previous bank of days for illness, there was a large sudden spike in medical procedures in the December before the change went into effect. The same pattern is evident for eyewear and dental care which have an annual or bi-annual allowance for services. Employees will hurry to use what is available before it expires.

Wages and Bonuses First

As we will see in later chapters, workers perform better when they see a direct tie between their work achievement and tangible rewards. This means they know what the company expects them to do, know what rewards they will receive as a result and, this is critical, perceive value in the reward. Unfortunately, when we substitute benefits for wages and bonuses, we penalize our best workers. Those who achieve the most, stay the healthiest and need minimal sick leave are being compensated the least, because a large chunk of their rewards are coming in a form they probably don't need.

Most businesses require workers to collaborate in teams, where one worker depends on several others. It isn't always easy for a manager to measure the exact contribution each one makes. Through a simple law of averages, inaccurate assessments of performance make it likely that a business will *undervalue top workers* and allow *low performers to remain undetected*. The more misaligned a company's pay structure is and the less accurately performance is monitored, the more it will favor hidden underperformers over top workers. Rewarding your best workers for their productivity means critically evaluating how and for what you pay people, and whether the *work-for-pay* exchange is aligned.

Misaligned Messages

Before we discuss aligned incentives, it is helpful to look at the ways our traditional employment policies are misaligned. How much employers spend, and on what they spend, sends a message about what is important and what is not. How well do traditional policies align the interests of workers with the company?

For a moment, release your assumptions about what companies *usually* do. Read the following policies and think about how they translate into messages about value. If money talks, what does it "say" at your company?

Policy A: No bonuses, but all receive standard cost-of-living increases.

> **Translation:** Top performers are not of any higher value to us than those who perform poorly.

> **Impact:** Our research shows that overall performance suffers in environments without performance-based rewards. In fact, high performers are more likely to leave jobs when they are not rewarded for performance.

Policy B: Pay is based on attendance, not output.

Translation: Face time is more important than what you do while you're here.

Impact: Like Policy A, when time is used as the proxy for productivity, we see lower production in all workers and higher turnover in top workers. Further, team morale and quality of life suffer when workers compete to be seen working early or late. If time is what earns pay, workers will make sure management sees their car in the parking lot late at night, even if no productive work has been done all day.

Policy C: Unlimited sick time (yes, this still exists), 100% pay during disability, and use-it-or-lose-it benefit plan designs.

Translation: You are worth as much to us when you're at home and ill as you are when you're working.

Impact: When workers earn the same amount of money whether they work or not, absence and work have equal value to them. Companies with use-it-or-lose-it policies on PTO and sick leave force employees to take as much time as they are given to receive full value.

Policy D: Rich medical and absence benefits without performance pay.

Translation: We pay our sickest people the most.

Impact: When bonuses and job training opportunities are sacrificed to fund health-related benefits, the workers who get the highest total compensation are those who use the most health services. A person heavily engaged in benefit utilization, whether sick or not, will get full pay, time away from work, and potentially hundreds of thousands of dollars in medical services. The high-performing well person will receive his regular base pay—and no more.

Policy E: No profit sharing.

Translation: We are not on the same team. Regardless of how successful the company is, your pay situation will not change.

Impact: Employees who feel that they have little connection to company success are less engaged, less productive, and less protective of corporate assets.

Clearly the messages above are unintentional. No employer sets out to de-value high performers or reward absenteeism. But in their antiquated attempts to "protect" employees against losses, businesses have instead created an unproductive work environment where showing up, working hard and staying healthy have less value. By mistake, today's business culture protects absence and poor performance at the expense of rewarding the best workers. Next, we'll examine what alignment means and how to achieve it.

Part 2

SAVING YOUR COMPANY

CHAPTER 2

ALIGNING INCENTIVES IN AN EFFECTIVE WORK CONTRACT

Align: to be on the side of or against a cause;
to fall into line; to be in correct relative position.

Opinion or Reality?

The influence of incentives, and by that we mean costs and benefits of all kinds, monetary and nonmonetary, tangible and intangible, has been well-documented in economics for centuries.[9] Nothing we present in this book will surprise market economists, although they may find our examples interesting.

This book is different because it takes some basic economic principles and applies them to human resources. The principles are not new. But they may give a new perspective about how companies can improve business performance. Alignment is not a philosophy or interesting new trend for productivity management.

---

9. Laffont, J. Martimort, D. The Theory of Incentives: The Principal-Agent Model. Princeton University Press. 2001.

It is a real force that affects employee behavior, whether businesses recognize it or not. Misaligned incentives are harming company performance today, and aligning them could fix what's wrong. Our message in this book is a simple one: when incentives for two parties are aligned, the results are more mutually beneficial and productive than when incentives are misaligned.

Workers are more productive, businesses are more successful, expenses are lower, and health and well-being are better when companies align the incentives and best interests of the company with those of the worker. Companies that align worker goals with corporate goals simply do better.

In work settings, companies want to maximize profits while workers want to maximize their own earnings and well-being. If incentives can be designed so that both parties can serve their own best interest through the same activities, for example, working hard or efficiently, results will be superior to when incentives encourage activities that serve only one party.

What Is Success?

What makes a company successful? From an outsider's point of view, success comes in the form of earnings per share, or greater market share; it's revenue, customer retention, and profit margin. Most would agree that over time, successful organizations need to:

- Attract and retain top talent
- Achieve high performance of workers and managers
- Increase profit margins
- Demonstrate high attendance/availability of employees
- Grow worker capacity
- Drive new and creative product design

These goals are achieved through the collective actions of many employees producing a coordinated set of results.

In reality, big successes happen because of small and marginal successes: one worker at a time, one day at a time, and one task at a time. Or more specifically, one worker, doing the right task, at the right time, in the most efficient way, keeping other objectives in mind, multiple times, every day.

Conservatively, a company of 100 people, working 250 days per year, will do one task per hour, working with five other colleagues. That's a *million* opportunities for success…or for failure each year. What makes success more likely in each of those million opportunities? Being aligned.

Aligned or Not?

Some business leaders assume that if they hire the right people with the right skills who fit into their corporate culture, success will follow. Not necessarily. We often compare similar companies with similar workforce characteristics. Frequently one is high performing and one stagnates. One has high worker attendance and low benefit costs, while the other requires over-staffing to cover high absence rates. If workers arrive with the same experience, education, and skills, what makes some of them thrive and the others falter? *Aligned interests. Aligned incentives.*

Aligning incentives means joining forces for a shared cause; at work that cause is shared success for both organization and worker. Are management and workers aligned? Are operations and human resources aligned? Are bosses and employees aligned? If not, expect inefficiencies, turnover and high costs. But if they are aligned, we see higher performance, prudent use of resources and greater bottom lines.

How much of a difference can alignment make? In aggregate (across many companies), we've seen differences like those shown in table 2:

Table 2: Effects of Aligning Incentives

Outcome	Effect of Aligning Incentives
Medical costs	$2,500 per person less per year
Short-term disability	50% lower rates
Workers' compensation	65% fewer total days
Turnover	50% lower in top performers
Revenue	35% higher
Productivity	20% higher

Subsequent chapters will outline key elements of alignment, consequences of misalignment and steps for realigning ineffective business practices. It's a summary of the key business lessons we've learned after years of research and consulting, boiled down into a few simple truths that your company can implement at very little expense, and yet you can expect to see measurable impact in less than a year.

Why Incentives Work

We wrote in much greater detail in a previous book[10] about the economic theories underlying alignment. Basically, the reason incentives work is because humans naturally act in their own best interest.

---

10. Lynch W., Gardner H. *Aligning Incentives Information and Choice*. Cheyenne, WY: Health as Human Capital Foundation, 2008.

- We protect our own resource more than someone else's.
- If something seems free to us, we consume more of it.
- What gets paid for is what gets done.
- Resources are finite, so more of one thing means less of another.

Simply: good and bad consequences for our behaviors will affect what we do. Thus, the more we align what an employee wants with what the company needs, the better both will do.

CHAPTER 3

CURRENTS: A METAPHOR FOR INCENTIVES

I magine that each company is a river with a smooth surface. New employees launch their boats and begin paddling toward company goals. From an observer's perspective, employees on one river may appear to be paddling hard but not making significant progress toward company objectives. He may conclude that these workers must lack motivation or paddling skill. On another river, which looks identical, our observer may see workers taking their boats quickly toward the desired destination with little obvious effort. "Ah," he perceives, "These must be the right kind of skilled, dedicated workers."

On the surface, underlying currents may not be visible. Anyone who has paddled in one knows that currents can be powerful: with us, the current propels us forward; against us, the current makes progress difficult. Staying still is almost impossible, because currents move us even when we aren't paddling ourselves.

Think of the policy-driven incentives faced by employees as a collective current pulling on workers at all times. Alignment is the degree to which currents flow in the same direction as company goals. If it seems that employees tend to drift toward undesirable outcomes (underperformance, high absenteeism, or turnover), then you can be sure incentives are making them drift that way. But the opposite is also true; aligned incentives draw employees toward positive behaviors and there is ample opportunity for employers to correct misaligned currents underlying the workplace culture.

Two Major Currents

There are two major currents: shared rewards and shared responsibilities.

Shared Rewards represent the sum of all ways that an organization shares positive business outcomes with employees. The most obvious example is sharing profits with employees in the form of bonuses. Strongly-aligned incentives in this category reinforce high achievement. We can also think of this as providing employees with "something to gain."

Shared Responsibilities represent the sum of all ways that an organization shares negative business outcomes with employees. An example here is paying less than a full day's wages to an employee who is away from work. Strongly-aligned incentives in this category reinforce efficiency and prudent use of resources. We can also think of this as employees having "something to lose."

A strong shared-rewards current will produce high performance as workers see a clear pathway to a win-win for both themselves and the business. This type of current will dramatically influence revenue and production. A strong shared-responsibility current will reduce unnecessary expenses. Workers see how waste and inefficiency come out of their own pockets. In a setting with a strong shared-responsibility current, absenteeism and benefit costs go down substantially.

These two types of currents do not always coexist. A company can have strong rewards without strong responsibilities. In that case, revenues are strong but expenses are high. When shared responsibilities are high without shared rewards, expenses are low but productivity lags. In Chapter 4, we will look at an alignment matrix of how rewards and responsibilities interact.

To maximize profitability, companies need both currents flowing steadily in the same direction, where the interests of the company and the interests of the employee are aligned. Let's look at each current in greater detail.

Shared Rewards

Over dinner one evening, our colleague was talking with her husband, "Chris," about work. His company sells medical supplies and he had recently been assigned new responsibility over accounts receivable (AR). Chris soon learned that AR was considered the "problem" department, often blamed for less-than-adequate collection rates and the employees perceived as poor performers overall. Unplanned absences were common. Chris saw that AR team members received very little feedback and what they did hear was uniformly negative and critical. Chris worried that the few high performers he had would not last long in such a difficult environment.

At this point in the conversation, the couple began brainstorming about what the environment would look like if they were to align incentives. The most important question: Were incentives aligned? Answer: actually, not at all. Regardless of how well or poorly the AR team performed, their pay and benefits stayed the same. Outstanding performance not only went unrecognized, it was lost in lackluster group totals. Team members shared no rewards when things went well and bore no accountability when they didn't. Performance didn't matter.

Hoping to Change the Currents, Chris Decided to Align Incentives

Looking over their past year's performance, Chris established a standard, achievable level of collections and two higher levels: high and exceptional. He sat down with the team and explained that AR staff would receive immediate feedback about collection rates and that rates exceeding high or exceptional levels would result in bonuses at the end of each month. In all, staff members could earn an extra 12%-15% of their base wage if their individual collection rates met the highest goal levels.

How Soon Did Behavior Change? *Day One*

Here were the instant effects:

- staff members became immediately more aware of their own (and team) performance levels and tracked performance daily;
- two poor performers, sensing the change in environment, quit;
- attitude and energy levels shifted positively.

Business Results?

Collections increased from an average of $1M per month to $1.35M per month. The amount of debt that remained uncollected each month decreased from almost 12% to under 3%. The gain to the organization resulted in a spike in profitability, prompting senior leadership to notice and inquire, "What happened?" For the first time, the AR department received positive recognition in the form of both performance pay and public praise for their contributions to business success.

How Do Shared Rewards Affect Benefits Utilization?

The side effect of shared rewards is often a shared sense of accountability. Once employees became eligible for performance-based bonuses, they also became acutely aware that days away from work would affect their own bottom line. Missing multiple days of work now carried a greater economic weight for everyone—the company and the individual.

The effect on sick leave is shown below in figure 5: the average number of unexpected absences per month for a team of 13 people went from 19 days (1.5 per person each month) to 6 days (fewer than .5 per person), almost a 75% reduction. This occurred without a change in formal absence policy, or an intervention to improve employee health. It occurred because being at work mattered more to members of the AR team.

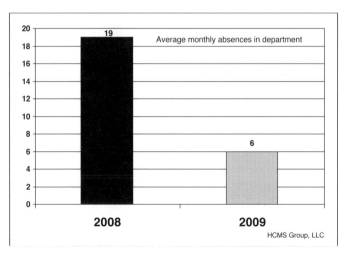

Figure 5: Reduction in absences after pay-for-performance bonuses

Here's the formula:

Intervention = Make health and attendance matter more by rewarding performance.

Result = Lower absenteeism, higher productivity, retention of three exceptional high performers (who Chris worried were ready to leave).

This example illustrates the role of economic incentives in a complex situation that was out of alignment. By placing a monetary value on specific work outcomes, workers not only saw greater opportunities for rewards, but also gained:

- clarity about specific expectations;
- regular feedback about performance;
- a mechanism for giving visibility to high performers;
- additional praise and recognition when things went well.

Obviously, all of these factors contributed to their amazing performance turn-around. But it started with a clear message about the value of good performance, in the form of money.

Shared Rewards Are About WIIFM… What's In It For Me?

As we described in the last chapter, shared rewards are all of the ways that employees have something to gain when positive outcomes occur for the organization.

Below we list seven business practices that contribute to shared rewards.

1. **Pay-for-performance**

   The most direct shared reward is pay that is tied directly to performance. This can come in the form of bonuses, profit sharing, or stock options. Another term for this is "variable pay," meaning it changes as performance or outcomes change.

We emphasize "variable pay" because often we speak with employers who insist *"we do pay bonuses."* However, the bonuses are given to every employee regardless of individual or team performance and in the same amount each year. This does not qualify as pay-for-performance or variable pay because performance does not affect the amount.

Key aspects of pay-for-performance:

a) It must be sufficient in size to influence behavior. Our data suggest that bonuses below 5% of regular wage send a positive message but have minimal performance impact. Performance rewards that are 10% of salary or more have a significant, measureable effect. We see even stronger effects at 20% of salary. As the amount of pay-for-performance increases, so does productivity. However at some point, larger bonuses may not add much in the way of incentives because the extra income does not produce proportionate increases in marginal utility to the worker.

b) It must be frequent enough to influence behavior. The more frequent it is, the more influential it will be. Monthly is ideal. Quarterly is good. Annual may suffice if necessary, or if measuring performance is very expensive. When pay-for-performance is measured and awarded across longer periods, then the goal is more to influence retention than to influence performance.

c) The metrics of performance must be tangible, reliable, and objective enough to influence specific behaviors. The employee must understand what accomplishment will produce the reward and believe that the measure is valid. Frequent or ongoing visibility of the metric itself reinforces continuous effort.

d) The best performance metric is based on elements that the individual can influence. Profit sharing is a positive pay-for-performance tool. However, some workers may feel disconnected from any ability to influence profitability or may not understand executive decisions to redirect profits into research and development.

e) Effective performance metrics include thoughtful combinations of goals. It is important to think through performance goals because *you will get what you pay for.* If goals are completely based on individual performance, workers may not help their team-members as much. If goals only reflect short-term results, workers may not consider long-term implications. For example, if short-term rewards discourage taking time for necessary training, it may sacrifice long-term improvements in performance.

2. **Cash back for unused paid time-off**

As we will discuss in the shared responsibility section below, paid time-off is probably the most misaligned of all business practices; intentionally exchanging full pay for doing no work.

If the company offers paid time-off, rewarding those who choose to use less of it is an aligned practice. Allowing individuals to choose to work more, at full pay, rather than insisting that they miss work to use the benefit, as is the case with use-it-or-lose-it policies, gives an appropriate reward for working.

3. Training allowances

Growth in skills and work capacity results in a mutual benefit for the worker and the company. Financing for work-relevant skills, such as tuition or a training allowance, reinforces that employee success and the company's success are strongly tied. These investments should represent a reward for past performance and an investment in future performance improvement.

4. Retirement deposits/matching funds, or deferred compensation

Employers benefit from having employees with financial security. Living paycheck-to-paycheck reduces the number of options people have and can trap them into unsatisfactory jobs or difficult life situations. Generous matching in 401K plans provides a cushion for employees to rely on in cases of emergency or, perhaps, allows them to make necessary changes in their career paths.

While some may consider it counterintuitive, having secure employees who can absorb unexpected events and expenses allows them to be more productive in all aspects of their lives, including work. Those who avoid problems and stay employed get rewarded with a growing nest egg for their use later in life.

5. Maximum deposits in health savings accounts

For those less familiar with these types of accounts, HSA stands for health savings account. HSAs accompany high-deductible health plans. Usually, the plans have lower premiums than low-deductible plans.

Funds in health savings accounts are portable and kept by the individual after they leave the organization. The funds are not taxed and can be used for health expenses until age 65 when they can be used for any purpose. Thus, they are similar to having an extra 401K account.

There are several benefits of fully funding an HSA. Because the individual owns the money, he or she will be more careful in prudent healthcare spending. Research shows that spending is almost ten percent lower, premium rates have grown at only one third the rate of traditional insurance, and employees pay more attention to their health using these plans.[11, 12] When employers contribute a significant portion or all of the new high deductible, there is no new or extraordinary risk to employees. Unspent funds roll over each year, thus rewarding workers over time for staying healthy. And the portion of those funds that would have been spent on higher premiums is put directly in the pockets of workers instead of going to insurance companies.

6. Coverage of preventive activities and screenings at 100%

In combination with health savings accounts, full preventive coverage classifies as a shared reward. Following the guidelines of the United States Preventive Services Task Force,[13]

11. Insurance Online Quotes. Keeping Your Health Insurance Premiums Low. May 18, 2010; http://insuranceonlinequotes.com/keeping-your-health-insurance-premiums-low/381/ (accessed Nov 15, 2010).
12. Hoewisch, K. Employers, Employees Save with a Good HSA Program Design. HR Management Nov, 2008; http://www.hrmreport.com/article/Employers-Employees-Save-with-a-Good-HSA-Program-Design/ (accessed Nov 15, 2010).
13. U.S. Preventive Services Task Force (USPSTF). Recommendations. http://www.ahrq.gov/clinic/uspstfix.htm#Recommendations (accessed Nov 15, 2010).

certain tests help to identify health problems early. Also, immunizations for such things as flu can effectively prevent outbreaks that strain a company and cause suffering and lost income for the individual.

7. Pay for extra effort in the form of time

The ability to earn overtime pay seems to produce some positive behaviors, such as greater attendance and greater attention to health. For example, we have seen that workers who are eligible for overtime are more likely to get flu shots to avoid losing the opportunity for overtime.[14]

Thus, the opportunity to work more can have its shared rewards. There are limits, however. Our data show that above certain amounts of work time, there may be safety or work effectiveness concerns.[15] Thus, it may be prudent to put limits similar to those for pilots and truck drivers on the amount of overtime per week one can earn.

Quick Score: Shared Rewards

How well does your company create a current of shared rewards? Check Yes in table 3 for each item that exists in your company, or for a certain group in your company.

Counting the number of Yes answers in the list gives an organization a quick shared-rewards score. While there are much more detailed ways of assessing shared rewards, these check boxes in table 4 give a quick sense of the strength of this current.

---

14. Health as Human Capital Foundation. Money Matters. What do skinny people in big houses have to do with flu shots and bonus pay? Entry 11 - 2008. May 26, 2008; http://hhcf.blogspot.com/2008/05/money-matters-what-do-skinny-people-in.html (accessed Jun 5, 2008).
15. Unpublished corporate data. HCMS Group.

Table 3: Shared rewards quick score

Does this condition exist for most employees? (Count the number of Yes answers)	Check if Yes
Employees are eligible for performance bonuses.	
If yes, employees know exactly how their bonuses are determined.	
Bonuses are at least partially determined by individual performance.	
The total amount employees can earn in bonuses or profit sharing is >10% of salary.	
Employees can cash-in some unused paid time-off at 100%.	
Preventive care and screenings are covered at 100% (no deductible).	
Are *both* of these true: Employees are offered a training or tuition allowance worth at least 2% of salary and >10% of employees use it.	
Are both of these true: Employees are offered a HSA with $2,000 or more in employer funds and at least 30% of employees choose this option.	
Employees receive a 401K deposit match at 4% or higher.	
All workers have multiple opportunities to increase skills and advance in the organization.	

Table 4: Shared rewards quick score implications

Score	Result	Implication
0 to 3	Misaligned	Productivity is 30%-40% below achievable. High turnover of top performers.
4 to 6	Neutral	Productivity and turnover will depend on other factors. When business climate is good, performance will be better. When climate is difficult, performance will suffer.
7 to 10	Aligned	Productivity is strong. Top performers stay.

This score indicates whether incentives are aligned to encourage high performance and to retain the top performers. Remember your score, because it will be used in later chapters.

EVIDENCE: DEFINING SHARED REWARDS

The simple checklist in this chapter evolved over many years, built on many studies and observations. It took time and data to verify which factors were important. Not surprisingly, some factors are more important than others and in some iterations (see note), each factor had a different weight depending on how strongly predictive it was of business outcomes. A weighted version might produce a more exact "score," but, in general, this 10-point score works well.

While virtually all policies in the list contribute to higher performance and better attendance, specific outcomes will be more associated with some items than others. For example, worker performance relates more to skills training than health accounts. Attendance will respond more to absence policies than retirement policies. From our evidence, all business outcomes respond most positively to well-designed bonus plans. The statistical modeling behind our shared-rewards score is quite remarkable. We took hundreds of thousands of people and created models that tested the effects of each of the individual policies (e.g., any bonus versus none, 401K amount, etc.) on each specific outcome (turnover, medical costs, disability, work performance). Then we tested each policy, controlling for other factors, which included age, gender, region of the country, salary, exempt status, marital status, and a few others, to see if the effect remained. If it remained, we then started combining multiple policies in the same models to see whether the combined effects produced a similar result.

Our team has run literally hundreds of statistical models over the past decade, testing all of these relationships between rewards and business outcomes. The results are what we simplified into our 10-point checklist. Shared rewards have more of an impact on productivity than other business outcomes, and bonuses have the most impact among all policies. However, they all matter.

Note: For anyone interested in a more sophisticated version that uses more detailed questions and more precise weighting, it can be found on the website at www.hcmsgroup.com.

Shared Responsibility

If two companies have identical workforces, with identical skills and identical health needs, does it matter what sort of benefits you provide? One would think that use of benefits depends on the needs of the workers covered. As long as benefit coverage is sufficient, the upper limit wouldn't matter, they just use what they need, right? Wrong.

If There Are No Limits On Sick Leave...

Consider this story from the *Wall Street Journal* in 2009.[16] In Belgium, the ministry of health reported that employees in some government departments average *35 days of sick leave per year.* The government pays full salaries for unlimited sick leave, which now totals almost 1.3% of GDP. Officials report that most workers on leave have been given a diagnosis of depression and that nothing can be done because, "you can't contradict the opinion of a psychiatrist." One expert estimates that only 5% are truly "cheating," but that at least 65% of those on government-paid leave could be working. However, they can't be forced back to work because they have a doctor's letter.

Employees in this scenario have learned that *they can get the same pay whether they work or not.* For employees who dislike their work, sick leave is a nice option, with no loss of income and no financial consequence. The work contract made this possible.

If You Offer Unusual Benefits...

Before becoming our client, one firm we consulted with decided to compete in their labor market by offering a richer benefits package than other major employers in the area. Their goal was to become an "employer of choice" through a superior benefits package. One such benefit was coverage for what is termed discretionary procedures, which are medical procedures that often have partial or restricted coverage by other plans.

In our work analyzing data for that employer, we discovered that their rate of bariatric surgery, commonly known as stomach

---

16. Miller JW. Belgians Take Lots of Sick Leave, And Why Not, They're Depressed. Wall Street Journal Online. January 9, 2009 http://online.wsj.com/article/SB123145414405365887.html (accessed November 15, 2010).

stapling or weight-loss surgery, was drastically higher than any other company we had seen. Not only that, but over half of those getting surgery quit the organization within 18 months! They had unintentionally become the employer of choice for the morbidly obese.

Remember: *the design of **pay** will attract the type of worker who values that form of **pay** the most.* In this example, people who wanted to use sick leave and have access to unusual benefits were drawn to this company. Unfortunately, workers whose primary goal was to be rewarded for high performance probably found this employer less attractive.

Something to Lose

Sharing responsibilities means putting some 'skin in the game'—aligning the interests of the worker with the interests of the company. Another way to think of them is "shared account-ability," or asking workers to be careful stewards of the resources made available to them. Below we list five business practices that create aligned incentives for shared responsibility.

1. **Pooled absence days for vacation and illness, or no PTO at all**

   Paid time-off (PTO) is one of the most misaligned practices in business—paying workers not to work. One way to share responsibility for time off is to combine sick leave and vaca-tion into one pool, or bank of days. If workers have freedom to use time off for any reason and can cash-in unused days, then they share responsibility for managing absence time.

   In our own firm, we do not offer any PTO other than national holidays. Instead, we pay 8%-10% higher wages, equivalent to 20 to 25 days out of the work year, and allow people to take as much unpaid time-off as they choose. In this way, we allow individuals to elect the amount of time off they prefer and do not attempt to dictate a "correct" number of days for everyone. Some employees take two weeks of time off; others take several months, but it's their choice.[17] Plus, because they aren't paid during absence, we do not ask them to carry a Blackberry, check-in or do work while they are away.

We have virtually no problem with attendance and, because performance bonuses are tied to profits, workers are mindful of both their productivity and excess costs. Employees are treated as adults in a business arrangement and, for the most part, they act that way.

2. **Reduced pay during extended illness**

   Many employers offer benefits that pay wages during extended illness absences. These can be in the form of salary continuance (no break in regular wages), short-term disability (STD) which usually lasts up to six months; and long-term disability (LTD) after a six–month absence. The terms of these benefits vary from full-coverage insurance, which covers 100% of wages, to offering options for employees to purchase minimal disability coverage.

   Our data suggest that at 100% pay during absence, employees file disability claims more often and stay out longer than at lower rates of pay. Figure 6 below graphs the rates of STD

---

17. Sometimes people ask how we manage loss of productivity for those who choose more time off. Clearly, long-term absences require significant planning and do not happen suddenly.

by age group, depending on the amount of pay covered in the first six months of absences.

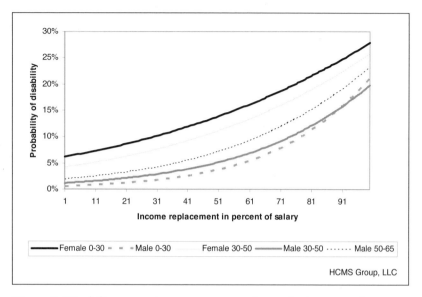

Figure 6: Disability events in non-exempt employees by income replacement in different age and gender groups

What we found was that the more a person is paid during absence, the more likely he is to become absent in the first place. One in five older, male workers earning 100% of salary for the first six-months of absence would be expected to file for disability. At 60% of salary, fewer than one in ten would be expected to file.[18]

Interestingly, certain medical issues are not sensitive to salary reimbursement. For example, claims for broken bones, which are virtually always a random, accidental event, are equally

18. Many people ask why female rates of spending are higher than male rates. A good portion of the difference is pregnancy-related and we retained pregnancy claims in this analysis. The primary point of the graph is to show that regardless of age or gender, more pay during absence results in a higher rate of extended absence.

likely to occur regardless of how much salary is covered during disability. However, claims for more ambiguous medical issues like back pain become more likely when more salary is covered. Based on this evidence, we advise employers to reduce coverage to below 100%, knowing that 80% coverage will reduce claims by about one-quarter, and 60% coverage will reduce claims by about one-half. Another powerful tool is to combine a lower STD reimbursement with a pay-for-performance bonus program. By combining "something to lose" with "something to gain," we multiply workers' incentives to return to work.

3. **High deductibles and OOP (out-of-pocket) max on health insurance, but no cost for premiums**

In the context of aligned incentives, health insurance coverage should reward good health and prudent use of medical services. It should not discourage getting coverage. Thus, to optimally align shared responsibilities, employers should cover healthcare premium costs, fully fund HSA accounts, supply health insurance with a large deductible that meets the HSA requirement or higher, and set a high out-of-pocket maximum (see Chapter 3 for more detail about the HSA).

These deposits in HSAs, along with generous accumulated savings from 401K plans, provide sufficient funds for individuals to cover unanticipated, catastrophic events, while strongly aligning incentives for staying healthy and managing health conditions effectively. Combining the generous funding of accounts and high-deductible health plan policies serves as both a shared reward (money saved for staying healthy and seeking care wisely) and a shared responsibility (sharing the cost when care is needed).

4. **Support for decision making in financial and health issues**

   If companies ask employees to share responsibility for making effective decisions regarding work, money and health, it follows that resources should be made available for informed decision-making. This includes access to unbiased information about medical options and unbiased information about financial options.

5. **Involvement in quality improvement efforts**

   One goal of aligned incentives is to encourage a shared-ownership mentality among workers and business leaders. Owners look for ways to improve output efficiency and effectiveness. Building a culture of continuous improvement, with a process for doing so, such as Lean Six Sigma programs or other similar efforts, encourages an ownership mentality at every level of the organization.[19] If the organization is going to share rewards and share responsibilities, then employees need the ability to make things run better. Now that success matters more, give everyone the tools to suggest and participate in improvements.

EVIDENCE: SHARED RESPONSIBILITIES

Most examples of shared responsibilities involve employers sharing costs either monetary cost or time, with employees. It shouldn't come as a surprise that when workers pay a greater share,

19. George M, Rowland D. Kastle B. *What is Lean Six Sigma?* New York: McGraw-Hill, 2004.

they use resources more carefully. However, what can surprise people is the size of the effect. Our best demonstration of the effects of shared responsibility came from an analysis we did comparing health costs among several companies.[20]

To model the independent effects of shared responsibility policies, we needed to isolate those effects from as many other factors as possible. So, we identified a sub-population in each company that had similar job functions: administrative workers. Then we included other factors we wanted to control in our models, including how long they had worked at their company, their gender, what region of the country they worked in, how many medical conditions they had, and what their health status was. Then we compared healthcare costs across companies, holding these factors constant.

This way we could answer the following question: if we look at female administrative workers, with an average work tenure of eight years, with an average of 3.8 health conditions, with same health status, living in the same areas of the country, what would we expect their annual healthcare costs to be in each of the companies? Figure 7 illustrates what we found.

The expected differences ranged from $2,705 to $4,981, a range of almost $2,300! We also measured their shared-responsibility scores and the rank order was the same. The company with the greatest shared responsibility (8 of 10) was #2, the company with the least shared responsibility (3 of 10) was #3. As you would expect, cost sharing for healthcare has the greatest impact on healthcare costs, and cost-sharing on time off has the greatest direct effect

---

20. Health as Human Capital Foundation.If we only consider one possible cause, we will be left with only one type of solution. Health status is not the only predictor of medical costs. Entry 5 – 2008. Mar 2, 2008; http://hhcf.blogspot.com/2008/03/if-we-only-consider-one-possible-cause.html (accessed Apr 27, 2010).

on absenteeism. However, they both have crossover effects on the other as well.

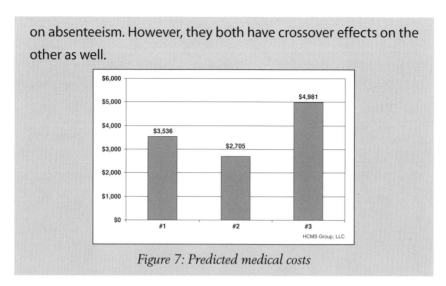

Figure 7: Predicted medical costs

Appropriate Levels of Responsibility

By sharing fiscal responsibility with employees, companies deliver a message that employment is a business arrangement. It is an exchange of pay, in many forms, for work. In the list above, we describe responsibilities that share some consequence but not a complete transfer of all risk. Employees will bear some of the cost, not all. Employees will experience some reduction in pay during extended absence, not lose all income. By sharing both positive and negative consequences, employees become conscientious stewards of the resources they are given.

A Question of Fairness?

Often, we hear reactions from employers that transferring any responsibility to employees is somehow unfair or harmful. Beneath these statements is more than a hint of paternalism and condescension, suggesting that employees do not have the capability or desire to be accountable for their *decisions that affect the profitability of the business.* One fact to remember: all benefits are paid for by employees. The employer may pay the service fee but funds for rising benefit costs come in lieu of paying employees higher wages (see Chapter 1). Additionally, only a small percentage of workers spend the majority of benefits dollars. In fact, less than five percent of employees use 50% of all medical and absences resources. Consequently, the workers who are at work, staying healthy and performing well will bear the ever-rising costs of the few who are not.

Thus, it is important to ask ourselves: do we truly believe that it's *fair* to take more and more pay out of employees' pockets to purchase benefits the majority of workers will not use in order to protect employees from themselves? Is this in the company's or the employees' best interest? Or have we as business leaders extended a paternalistic judgment about what we believe is best for everyone else? Beyond a certain level of protection or subsidy for services that employees cannot get on their own, decision makers have to consider the value of adding even *more* protection. More coverage for medical care or absence requires taking more pay from workers who perform well to provide more benefits, possibly to workers who don't perform as well. Is this a worthwhile tradeoff?

Quick Score: Shared Responsibility

As in the previous chapter, score your company's shared responsibility current. From the list of business practices in table 5, count the number of Yes answers.

Counting the number of Yes answers in the list gives your organization a quick shared-responsibility score. While there are much more detailed ways of assessing shared responsibilities, these check boxes in table 6 do give a sense of the strength of this current.

Table 5: Shared responsibility quick score

Does this condition exist for most employees? (Count the number of Yes answers)	Check if Yes
A pay statement clearly identifying the dollar value of all investments/benefits the organization makes on their behalf.	
A PTO bank of time off, rather than separate sick leave, vacation, etc.	
Less than 100% of pay during short-term and long-term disability.	
A company-wide, high-deductible health plan, with the deductible at least $2,000 to $4,000 (individual/family).	
An out-of-pocket maximum of $3,000/$6,000 (individual/family) or higher.	
Fewer than 31 days of paid time-off per year including holidays (but options for unpaid time).	
Active use of a quality improvement process (such as Lean Six Sigma) at all levels of the organization.	
A culture encouraging independent decisions about work.	
Resources for financial decision-making provided.	
Resources for healthcare decision-making provided.	

Table 6: Shared responsibility quick score implications

Score	Result	Implication
0 to 3	Misaligned	Avoidable healthcare utilization up to 30% higher regardless of health status. High absenteeism and disability rates.
4 to 6	Neutral	Healthcare utilization and absenteeism will be influenced by other factors, such as business climate.
7 to 10	Aligned	Prudent spending of healthcare dollars. Lower avoidable cost. Minimal excess or unplanned absences.

This score indicates whether incentives are aligned to encourage workers to use resources prudently and avoid unnecessary spending. Remember your score, because it will be used in the next chapter.

CHAPTER 4

THE ALIGNMENT MATRIX

Currents Can Strengthen or Contradict One Another

What is your corporate culture like? How do currents influence your work environment? If we plot shared rewards and shared responsibilities on a matrix, we create a diagram that describes the combined effects of overall incentive alignment. Are these currents working together, combining their aligned or misaligned effects, or do they create a mismatch of contradictory incentives? In figure 8, we've labeled the type of employer-employee relationship that is created by the currents inherent in a company's business practices. Along the vertical axis is the strength of the organization's shared-reward current. Along the horizontal axis is the strength of the company's shared-responsibility current. In this matrix we use the quick score from Chapter 3 to get a score ranging from 0 to 10.

Four Quadrants

Figure 8 describes and quantifies four types of 'corporate culture' employers have created with their business practices. Starting with the top right quadrant and going clockwise, the four are shown in table 7.

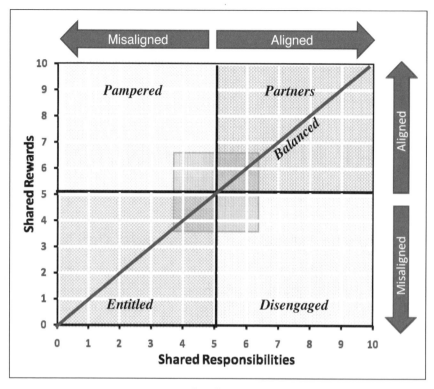

Figure 8: The alignment matrix

Table 7: Alignment matrix category definitions

Label	Rewards	Responsibilities	Expected Outcome
Partners	Aligned	Aligned	High performance Low expenses
Disengaged	Misaligned	Aligned	Low performance Low expenses
Entitled	Misaligned	Misaligned	Low performance High expenses
Pampered	Aligned	Misaligned	High performance High expenses

Identifying which quadrant best describes your organization allows you to understand why employees are performing the way they are and how to improve business outcomes.

In our experience, aligned business practices found in the Partner category are the most effective for achieving optimal business success. However, as we will explain, not all companies *choose* to align their business practices to achieve a Partner culture. We have spoken to business leaders who purposefully retain a Pampered culture because it fits their historical reputation in attracting workers. The same companies virtually *always* struggle with high benefit costs but their leaders have consciously chosen that tradeoff.

In any case, now an organization's leaders have the ability to understand why they are experiencing certain employee behaviors, such as high absenteeism, low performance, high turnover, etc., and make changes as they see fit.

Incentives in Action: What Companies Look Like in Each Quadrant

Company 1—Partner: My Success Is Your Success

True partnership occurs when all parties share the same goals, making all incentives aligned. Aligning both rewards and responsibilities creates a powerful current toward high performance and appropriate conservation of resources. Employees who have this type of employment agreement (see X1 in the fig. 9 matrix) have heightened awareness of how well the company is doing (it's their earnings, too!) and find ways to spend less on benefits that they may or may not value.

In our own firm, we attract high-performing employees who have very low benefits spending (our insurer actually reduced our health insurance premiums in 2010)[21] and who have very low turnover. As you might expect, strong shared-reward and shared-responsibility currents mean our employees are personally affected by the performance of the company and consider themselves partners in its success.

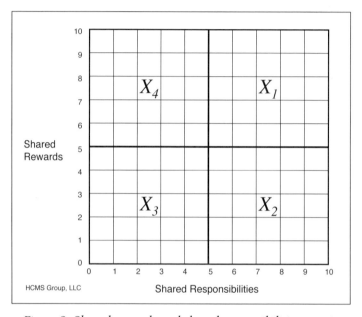

Figure 9: Shared rewards and shared responsibilities matrix

Company 2—Disengaged: Don't Expect Much

In the bottom right quadrant (fig. 9), employers have created a culture where neither party expects much from the other. This may be "contract" or "temp" workers, or industries that offer hourly work with minimal benefits. Here, pay usually rewards hours spent, with little opportunity for bonuses, training, or other opportunities

---

21. Some may interpret this to mean that we only hire "healthy" people. Not so. First of all, that is illegal. Second of all, illnesses happen to everyone. Actually, our employees have experienced many health issues, some as serious as cancer. However, employees pay attention to their spending and use care prudently.

for enhancement of human capital. Additionally, benefits include low levels of paid time-off and little healthcare coverage.

These arrangements are relatively low risk for employers; however, they are also unlikely to inspire high performance or loyalty. We applied the label "disengaged" because neither party is likely to have great interest in the success of the other. While employers avoid high expenses from benefits, they may battle the cost of high turnover.

Company 3—Entitled: The Pay Is Lousy, But The Benefits Are Great

Organizations in this quadrant often include government agencies. The culture probably resembles that of your own state, county, or city employees. The sad reality of public employment is that without business objectives to achieve (usually the model is simply to spend what budget one is given and the more the better) or profits to earn, employment contracts have largely misaligned incentives. Most public agencies reward attendance and seniority, emphasizing compensation types other than pay. Public employees often receive huge amounts of time off (because the direct cost of time off is low), rich pensions (which are guaranteed by self-invested legislatures), and few, if any, opportunities for performance bonuses or other rewards because performance outcomes are difficult to define or measure. If we follow the rule that employment contracts attract the type of workers who value them most, these jobs will attract workers who, in general, value long-term employment, rich health benefits and extensive time off more than financial rewards for hard work. Certainly this does not mean that ALL workers in this sector are unmotivated, simply that risk-taking entrepreneurs looking for high-earnings opportunities do not seek this type of *pay* package.

In our matrix (fig. 9), public employers often fall into the bottom left quadrant (see X3) in the entitled category. This group is characterized by having *both* currents misaligned, producing low performance and high benefits use. There is little incentive to work hard and little incentive to spend one's resources carefully. Business success simply doesn't matter very much.

Company 4—Pampered: Hire the Best and Spoil Them

This company philosophy is taken from another company with whom we have worked. Their attitude has been: We hire the best, most highly trained workers in the high-tech industry. We expect them to work very long hours under intense stress, so we don't want them to have to worry about anything else. We make sure our health benefits are second to none—including coverage for alternative medicine, chiropractic care and other perks.

As you can imagine, this company has strong shared rewards; a score of 8 out of 10 (shown as X4 in fig. 9). Worker productivity is stellar and employees are rewarded with bonuses and stock options. This company does attract and retain high performers. But shared responsibilities are almost nonexistent (2 out of 10). As a result, they fall high in the top left corner of the pampered quadrant. The consequences of a pampered employee culture are not minor. This organization has the highest combined medical and absence expenditures of any group we have studied, despite having a relatively young, healthy, high-performing population.

In fact, when we did a statistical analysis of their expected costs, holding constant factors such as job, salary, tenure, health status, etc., we calculated that they *cost more than double* what we have seen for employees in similar jobs. The reason: incentives. Employees at this organization are told to spare no expense, that they deserve every visit to the massage therapist they want and not to worry about it. In this case, the organization has made a conscious decision to have a pampered culture; leaders believe that the extra investment in additional benefits is worth the assumed return in loyalty and productivity. In other words, keep 'em happy, whatever it costs.

It's of note that recent economic pressures have disrupted the pampered culture at this employer somewhat. Not unlike spoiled kids used to getting their way, workers at this organization were shocked when the economic downturn led to a reduction in perks and vocalized their displeasure. Because they are not accustomed to thinking like 'owners' or 'partners,' they are less willing to share consequences for the bad times as well as the good times.

Alignment and Balance

When you align employment agreements it creates both a strong upside *and* a noticeable sense of responsibility for both parties. Some employers may decide to strengthen their shared-responsibility incentives to save money, without equally strengthening employee rewards. But doing one without the other may cause more harm than good. Balance is critical. Realignment involves reallocating and reinvesting resources, *not* reducing cost for the sake of short-term savings while ignoring the incentive climate. In fact, some realignment of rewards may involve *more* short-term spending, as the company shares additional revenue with workers. But the long-term effect is a win-win.

A key message: When you align incentives,
shared responsibilities should transfer directly
into larger shared rewards.

When aligning incentives, consider taking every dollar saved through shared responsibilities and reallocate it into a potential performance reward or training program. Put money left from lower premiums into HSA accounts. Put money saved on PTO into cash-back for unused days. As we see from the quadrants in figure 8, the ideal balance includes both aligned rewards and aligned responsibilities, without a heavy dose of one over the other. Money earned from enhanced business success should translate into tangible rewards for employees, especially if leaders intend to create a genuine and lasting culture of partnership.

EVIDENCE: MATRIX, MOTIVATION AND RESOURCE USE

The rewards and responsibilities matrix evolved after we noticed that companies often had separate philosophies about these two forms of incentives. One company would share rewards but assign workers no responsibilities; others would design high levels of cost-sharing but share no rewards whatsoever. The results were compelling, and gave us the ability to accurately predict the challenges a company was likely to face (high cost, low productivity, high turnover) just by knowing its scores.

It would follow, then, that the same incentives that define where a company falls in the matrix also influence the perceptions of employees. Our 2007 survey verified this for us. Regarding shared rewards, respondents who reported that good work was rewarded and recognized by their company (described in the "Evidence: Bonus" box in Chapter 1) were less likely to say that their own productivity suffered due to low motivation compared to respondents whose companies did not reward and recognize good work. They were also less likely to report that their coworkers' low morale reduced productivity.

For shared responsibilities, survey respondents having more and richer health-related benefits reported lower productivity. They also were more likely to report that "coworkers sometimes use disability benefits because they don't like their job," that "part of the reason I keep my job is for the benefits," and that "sick leave is part of benefits so I will make sure I use the days I have." All of these attitudes reflect what we know from our aggregate data analysis: shared rewards improve motivation to perform and shared responsibilities reduce the tendency to misuse resources.

CHAPTER 5

ALIGNED INCENTIVES IMPROVE PERFORMANCE AND REDUCE MODIFIABLE COSTS

With aligned incentives, work output increases substantially. If incentives are accompanied by a well-defined *work-for-pay* contract, you get substantial increases in output that matters. Workers in our example in Chapter 3 increased their accounts receivable revenue by 35% in the first month *as incentives were put into place*. A windshield-replacement firm that switched from paying hourly to paying per-windshield increased work output by 40% without sacrificing quality.[22] In example after example, we see that when we reward people for doing good work and clearly define what that is, performance improves dramatically. Our own analysis of the effect of aligned

---

22. In this example, each worker was assigned to fix any windshield that they, personally had incorrectly installed without additional compensation, reducing the incentive to work quickly while ignoring quality. Lazear EP. Performance pay and productivity. Am Econ Rev 2000;90(5):1346-61

currents has found that shared rewards in the form of variable pay will increase productivity by at least 1%-2% for each percent increase in variable pay (see table 8).[23]

Table 8: Estimated effect of alignment on employee performance

Alignment	Estimated effect on performance
Pay-for-performance	Up to 35% improvement
Avoided absence	2% performance improvement for each avoided week of absence
Training	6% improvement for every 10% of employees receiving training

Aligned Absence Policies

Although not as powerful as variable pay, aligned absence policies also improve productivity. At the very least, such policies reduce the amount of time a person is paid for not working (i.e., getting paid but producing zero value). These policies also reduce the rate of unplanned absences that disrupt the productivity of colleagues who depend on the absent worker. Unsurprisingly, when workers are paid less during absence (such as disability payments under 100% of salary), they return to productive work more quickly, requiring fewer replacement workers. Divided in equal amounts, each work week represents about 2% of a year. Thus, each absence day avoided can represent 0.4% productivity at a minimum. Avoiding a few sick days or use-it-or-lose-it days for each person adds up quickly across the organization.

---

23. In our database, we have used regression analyses to correlate outcomes such as revenue-per-square foot per retail employee with variable pay. We consistently find a measureable relationship between variable pay and improved performance.

Training

Employees who have better work skills will experience an improvement in productivity as well. The best estimate we have seen is that for each 1% of the workforce receiving meaningful training, productivity increases by 0.6%.[24] Like variable pay, training is a reward that produces higher productivity and is aligned with the interests of the organization.

Net Value

Obviously, people who work more, have better skills, and get bigger bonuses will be paid more. We often get questions about whether increases in revenue will simply be absorbed by higher pay for employees. The answer is no. Designed in the right way, employees improve output by a value greater than that which they receive in increased compensation, over and above the cost of training.

For example, training studies indicate that training increases wages by 0.3% while increasing productivity by 0.6% on average. In our accounts receivable example, workers increased their incomes by about 15%, while increasing revenue by 35%. Similarly, the windshield installers increased wages by as much as 28%, while increasing production by an average of 40%.

In total, we can calculate a 40%-50% increase in worker output for organizations that are completely aligned compared to those that are completely misaligned. Depending on the type of business, this will translate into different levels of actual profitability. But each misaligned incentive that a company realigns will increase

---

24. Dearden, L. Reed, H., Van Reenen, J. The Impact of Training on Productivity and Wages: Evidence from British Panel Data. Centre for Economic Performance. CEP Discussion Paper No 674. February 2005.

worker output while reducing costs. In the next section, we'll outline how to measure the portion of your current costs that are modifiable through alignment.

How Much Can We Reduce Expenses?

As we have seen, misaligned incentives encourage over-use of absence and healthcare benefits. We used our large, integrated database to quantify just how much over-use is due specifically to misalignment. We modeled patterns of utilization across hundreds of thousands of employees, controlling for health-related factors.[25] We used a statistical analysis to divide costs into two major categories: non-modifiable costs and modifiable costs. We combined all health-care costs with absence, disability and workers' compensation costs.

Non-Modifiable Cost

For all companies, there are costs of doing business, a minimum of employee expenses that will be incurred in the best of circumstances. They are:

1. Lowest possible essential costs and bad luck

Here we looked at the costs of healthcare and absence for young, healthy, highly educated, (single) male workers[26] living in inexpensive areas of the country. In other words, these are people for whom we would expect only accidental

---

25. This analysis controlled for employee age, gender, geographic region, salary, as well as severity of illness and number of medications.

26. While some might object to our selection of only young males as a "base," the reality is that women do have more expenses than men, mostly due to childbearing. The point is not to suggest that hiring young (unmarried) men is preferable, but simply to point out that demographics—gender, age, location, and other factors—influence cost. When we hire workers with experience and skill, they will have various characteristics: younger, older, healthier and less healthy. As readers will see in the next section, the most effective way to manage cost is through incentive alignment, regardless of workforce demographics.

or routine health problems, no pregnancies and few chronic illnesses. This is the *best possible hypothetical* experience we could imagine, and one that no company can achieve. Thus, it is considered a non-modifiable, best case. Every other case will involve adding costs to this best-possible amount.

Cost: about $1,300 per year.

2. Demographic and labor pool influences

If we take a more typical, young group of employees (male and female) in the Northeast (where costs are high), we would estimate their additional cost from demographics and location to be about $900 per person. This includes added cost from aging, childbearing, living in various parts of the country (where people live different lifestyles and have different costs for healthcare), lower wages, job type, education, and any other personnel factors.

To give a sense of how demographics affect cost, see table 9 below. Keeping the same region (Northeast), we see an almost four-fold difference in expected cost for this category as age changes. Thirty-year-olds can be expected to have an average demographic and labor cost of $900. Sixty-year-olds

Table 9: Total non-modifiable employee costs

Non-Modifiable	Age 30	Increase age to 40	Increase age to 50	Increase age to 60
Basics and bad luck for a young, healthy workforce	$1,300	$1,300	$1,300	$1,300
Demographics and labor pool	$900	$1,700	$2,300	$3,400
Total non-modifiable	$2,200	$1,300	$3,600	$4,700

can be expected to have almost four times the demographic and labor cost ($3,400).

Adding both basic and demographic costs together, we get a total that essentially calculates what an employer can expect to pay if the company stays in the same industry and same general location, recruiting from the same labor pool. Depending on the age, gender, type of workers and region, non-modifiable costs may range from a low of about $2,200 to a high of near $5,000.

Modifiable Cost

As this book emphasizes, despite the essential costs of doing business, there is an extraordinary portion of workforce spending that can be improved or at least modified and which is unique to each business. The two types of modifiable cost are:

1. Health status cost

Once again, to isolate the influence of health, we hold constant basic needs, bad luck, demographics, and labor pool factors described above. In the end, our research finds that a 10% improvement in health will influence and reduce costs by about the same amount, between 7%-11%.

Here is what we mean:

- A 10% improvement in self-reported health status (a 10% shift to a higher score on a scale of poor to excellent) corre-lates with a combined medical and disability cost decrease of approximately the same amount, 9%.

- A 10% decrease in the number of diagnoses people have correlates to a medical and disability cost reduction of 11%.

- A 10% decrease in the number of medications people need results in a medical and absence cost reduction of 7%.

These analytic models tell us that when health-related metrics indicate that a population is 10% healthier than average, they will be about 10% less costly. If the population is 20% healthier, we would expect them to be 20% less costly. This can be very surprising to those of us who were taught to believe that the major driver of cost is health status; and that the only way to reduce cost is to improve health. In essence, this tells us that bad luck plays a part, aging (things wearing out) plays a part, and the healthcare delivery system plays a part. Below we will see that one of the biggest causes of higher costs is misaligned incentives.

2. Misaligned incentives or business practices

Compared to health status, the impact of misaligned incentives is usually large. While it might be possible to improve overall costs by 10%-20% by improving health, the "average" company with very poor incentive alignment could reduce costs by three to four times that amount. We often see $1,300-$1,400 of excess costs simply due to bad business practices and misaligned incentives, up to 30% of total benefit costs. And yet, we have seen misalignment-related costs as high as 50% of total! One company had *average* excess costs of over $12,000 per person. We predicted that their costs could be reduced to $6,000 with aligned incentives. Happily, we can also report that a company with well-aligned incentives had a predicted misalignment cost of zero.

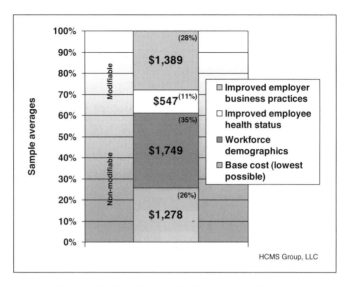

Figure 10: Medical and absence cost drivers

Total Modifiable Costs

Figure 10 comes from modeling a "typical" firm among many with whom we have worked. Total medical and health-related absence costs for an individual employee are approximately $5,000, of which almost 40% is modifiable. Improving health significantly (eliminating one in ten diseases) would decrease costs by about 10%. Aligning incentives would decrease costs by almost 30%. What would it take to achieve that 30% reduction? Simply implement most of the shared rewards and shared responsibilities we described in Chapter 3.

Strategic Business Implications

For businesses looking to strategically focus on their modifiable costs, the implications of the research here are striking. For all of the resources and investment that often go into health and wellness programming, the total potential for cost reduction is about

10%—*if the program works.* Improvements to policy alignment however, require very few, if any, vendor contracts or program fees and often cost no new money, just redistribution of current spending. Yet the potential cost savings from internal business practice alignment is 30%, nearly three times the best possible impact of buying external wellness programs!

As we saw earlier in this chapter, aligned incentives increase top-line performance. Here we see aligned incentives also reduce expenses, including medical costs, absences, and avoidable injuries. The result: a better bottom line overall.

Objections To Alignment

Aligning incentives requires changing some of your existing policies. Change can be scary. Here are some responses to common concerns we hear.

Worry: *We have to offer rich benefits to attract the best workers!*

Flaw: Attracting good workers by offering lavish benefits is like attracting a spouse by offering a lavish lifestyle. After you get him, will he be married to you for the right reasons? One has to wonder if disability insurance, time off, and medical and dental coverage are more important to a job candidate than profit sharing or advancement opportunities. What does that suggest after he is hired? Even if he has a great resume, will his idea of satisfying employment fit yours?

Employers can offer a lucrative employment agreement without creating counterproductive, misaligned currents. For example, offering higher performance bonuses, more training, and advancement opportunities maintains alignment while increasing value to the employee.

Worry: *What if employees quit because we change our benefit package?*

Flaw: Assuming that your best workers are here primarily because of benefits.

The answer to this question depends on which employees you are concerned about. Top performers quit for different reasons than poor performers. We have analyzed the effects of business practices and policies on turnover rates across many companies. The basic answer is this: top workers want to be noticed, recognized, and rewarded for superior performance with bonuses and opportunities. If their level of shared rewards and opportunities accomplishes this, they tolerate increased responsibilities. This is especially true if they understand clearly how money from benefits is being reallocated into better opportunities for them in terms of pay.

Low performers want to avoid being noticed, recognized, or rewarded less for unsatisfactory performance. They may have chosen a job because of benefits, which is not an uncommon way to get healthcare coverage these days. In our research, such workers are more likely to quit after realignment. In our example in Chapter 3, where performance soared after bonuses were offered, the two lowest performers quit immediately. Three top performers, who had previously been unhappy, stayed and thrived. Other companies have reported similar trends, where top workers stay because they feel more valued and rewarded.

Worry: *What if we don't provide "enough" time off to let employees balance their lives?*

Flaw: There is no single type or level of employee benefit that is "best" or "right" for all employees.

In most situations, employers have options regarding the level of each benefit to provide (how much vacation, what level of disability coverage, etc.). There is no correct level that fits all employees equally well. A fall-back position worth considering is to cover a basic plan with an option to select more coverage at the employee's expense.

Worry: *But we will get bombarded by complaints!*

Flaw: Believing that satisfaction with benefits is more important than aligned rewards.

Sticking with tradition or avoiding complaints is not reason enough to maintain a misaligned benefits-design strategy. More than any other tendency in this list, we see employers setting policy based on complaint-avoidance. While most express fear about losing top workers who get angry about policy changes, in reality, true-realignment will favor high performers. Thus, complaints, if any, will likely come from poor performers. Some may consider complaints to be an indicator of low morale. We might argue that those complaints usually reflect a minority of workers and usually the least engaged to begin with. However, aligning incentives is most likely to decrease the morale of low-productivity workers, while increasing the morale of high-productivity workers. One might question whose morale is most important?

If you find yourself or others objecting to a specific business practice, examine why. Is it because your company believes in the paternalistic goal of protecting workers from making bad decisions? Is it because you are afraid of losing good workers? Or is it because you fear a flood of complaints? Are your concerns warranted? On what basis?

Worry: *Rewards based on individual performance are unfair and undermine teamwork.*

Flaw: "Fairness" practices, or paying everyone the same amount, favor the worst performers and discourage top performers. Practices that give all employees equal value by definition favor those who produce the least work. So, who is actually being treated unfairly? It is possible to reward employees based on both team and individual goals so that employees gain value from doing well and working together. These are not mutually exclusive.

Often, resistance to a more alignment-based approach stems from anecdotal stories of negative consequences rather than concrete examples where companies measured the outcome of implementing a new business practice. Fear of a mass-exodus of disgruntled workers is a powerful deterrent to change. But realignment, when designed for mutual benefit, can and does produce positive results for companies and workers alike.

It is possible to reward people for both individual and corporate performance in ways that promote hard work and teamwork without creating unnecessary stress or counterproductive competitiveness.

Worry: *Misalignment isn't the problem. Our policies may be misaligned, but the **real** reason our costs are high is because our employees are just sicker than employees at other companies.*

Flaw: A business practice will attract the type of worker that particular practice benefits most.

Workers will seek an employment contract that matches what they value most. If an employee wants to be well rewarded for being a high performer, he or she will seek an environment with significant bonuses. If an employee wants job security and a lot of time off, he or she will seek a job with that package. High-cost employees are more likely the product of benefit design and self-selection than illness level.

Worry: *We don't think realignment can fix our poor performance problem*

Flaw: Perceiving performance to be the fault of the worker, rather than a consequence of your incentive misalignment.

By definition, poor performance means that workers do not meet the expectations of a work contract in a manner sufficient to earn their compensation. In other words, their *work* does not warrant their *pay*.

More often than not, we find that poor performance results from flaws in the work contract, not because workers aren't able to perform well. Common problems are:

- Elements and expectations about work are poorly defined.
- Worker skills did not fit work requirements when hired.
- Workers receive inadequate feedback to improve their work.
- Workers were attracted to the job for other aspects of pay than performance rewards.
- Incentives are misaligned so that worker interests are in conflict with the interests of the company.

When incentives are realigned and clearly contained in a work contract, poor performers have a much higher chance of succeeding.

Part 3

A STEP-BY-STEP METHOD
TO FIX THE WORK CONTRACT

CHAPTER 6

MEASURING WORK VALUE

A Different Sort of Metric: Net Diem

How much is an employee worth to your organization? How much value does one person produce? And which investments increase that value? We use a measure to examine worker value that we call *net diem*, which is the net revenue a worker produces for each day he or she is paid. In its simplest form net diem is determined by:

> **Revenue generated minus all pay and benefits**
> ―――――――――――――――――――――――――
> **Number of paid days**

Conceptually, the equation tells us obvious ways to achieve greater net value. Other things being equal, workers generate greater net value when they:

- Generate more revenue
- Receive less pay and benefits
- Are paid for fewer days

The equation also suggests some other *aligned* ways to increase net value:

- Award pay in forms that result in higher revenue (such as training or bonuses) to counteract the expense.
- Reduce the number of days a person is being paid while not generating revenue.

Table 10 shows the items included in calculating net diem.

Table 10: How to calculate net diem

Aspect	Includes
Revenue	Actual revenue or presumed revenue equivalent of work achieved.
Pay	All forms of compensation including wages, bonuses, benefits and training.
Paid days	Number of paid days in a time period including paid days-off for sick leave, vacation or holidays.

An Illustration

A retail company wanted to track performance by department in four different stores. As we see in figure 11, net diem varied over time and between stores across a 10-month period. The difference between the top- and bottom-performing stores was almost $1,000 per day per person.

Further analysis revealed specific team characteristics accounting for the differences. Some could be expected: for example, teams with newly-hired employees generated less revenue as these new employees "learned the ropes."

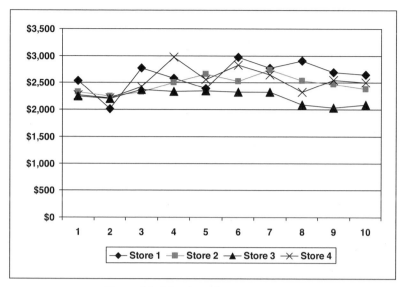

Figure 11: Net diem for existing stores

Interestingly, teams having more workers with ten years or more of tenure also had lower net diem. The reason was interesting: even though tenure contributed to higher revenues (these were talented sales representatives), after ten years, workers earned significantly more paid time-off (an example of a misaligned incentive). Thus, longer-tenured teams were paid more for time spent not working, which means they were paid for time when they were unproductive.

Net diem is most useful as a relative metric to compare performance between similar groups or similar employees, as seen in figure 11. It has less relevance comparing industries, especially when there are vastly different pay structures or profit margins in each.

Net diem can also be used to track performance in certain conditions. In figure 12, we see the same department with four new stores added. With each store opening, the department took several months to reach similar net diem levels; some had quicker success than others.

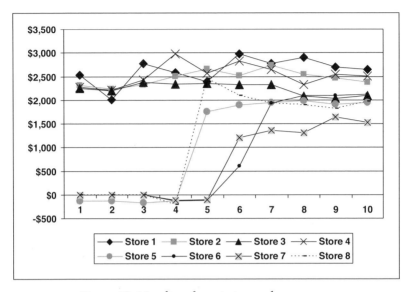

Figure 12: Net diem for existing and new stores

As we see here, before the departments began collecting revenue, their net diem numbers were negative, indicating full expenses with no revenue in the numerator.

A starting place for net diem can be at the full corporate level: total revenues minus total human capital expenses, divided by all paid days. This can be used to illustrate exactly how much value each employee must generate each day to maintain company profitability.

Net Diem As a Performance Metric

We created net diem because we found no other metric that quantified performance within the context of aligned incentives in the *work-for-pay* contract. It accounts for more factors than a revenues-to-salary ratio. For example, it directly takes into account the full cost of benefits by subtracting them from revenue, and it shows the value *lost* on each day that a worker is paid for *not* working. Another utility of net diem is that it forces companies to consider whether another dollar spent on *pay*, in all its forms, will either produce at least another dollar in revenue, or attract and retain high performers. Thus far, our analysis shows that of all the items included in *pay*, performance-based bonuses have the greatest positive return in net diem. In other words, a dollar spent on performance bonuses returns more than its value in increase revenue and reduced absences.

The example illustrated in figures 11 and 12 used team output to assess performance. While this is inferior to measuring individual performance, it was still very informative for the organization to compare similar teams across the organization and to learn what sorts of incentives and worker characteristics predicted better performance. Short-sighted methods for improving net diem are likely to backfire. A company with a disengaged culture that reduces bonuses or training to inflate the numerator would likely lose revenue-producing employees in the long run. Only careful selection of revenue-enhancing investments will increase the numerator and show that more value is produced, in net, each day. In a pampered culture, misaligned benefits policies will erode the value of high revenue as employees spend more on healthcare and take more PTO.

EVIDENCE: A MEASURE OF VALUE

There are many, many metrics used in the business world to reflect value. Financial measures reflect revenues, cash flow, and efficiency. Health programs usually try and measure value using return on investment before and after the program starts. After trying several different existing measures, we realized that nothing translated the performance of individual workers taking into account the exchange of work for pay. Further, company leaders rarely think about paid-time-off as a factor in individual-worker value, but they should. The number of days a company pays workers for not working does influence net value of work. While few companies will stop providing paid time-off, its effects should be clearly understood.

For our own clients, one of the first reports we often deliver quantifies the percent of "unproductive" time workers spend in the company. It would be an understatement to say that this report can come as a shock. If you tally all paid workdays including sick time, vacation, leave, disability, and workers' compensation, *plus* acknowledge that new workers take a few months to be fully productive and quitting workers often stop working as hard before they leave, the number can be quite large. In one firm, we calculated that over 28% of all compensation was being paid for unproductive time. Over 20% was being paid to workers when they were not working.

Net diem takes into account the value a worker produces, what the company spends to employ the worker, and adjusts it to account for absence. We know of no metric that more clearly illustrates the full exchange involved in the work contract.

CHAPTER 7

STEPS TO BECOMING ALIGNED

So, if we have convinced you that aligning incentives will help your business, here are some ways to move forward.

Step 1: Assess Your Alignment Today

First, understand which of your existing business practices are aligned and which are misaligned. The shared rewards and shared responsibilities quick score in Chapter 3 and the Alignment Matrix in Chapter 4 are a good start. If you want more detailed diagnostic information, talk to someone who specializes in incentive assessment. For example, our firm (www.hcmsgroup.com) runs a free incentive diagnostic that collects information and quantifies the size of realignment opportunities.

Get a clear understanding of the strength of both currents: shared rewards and shared responsibilities. Determine where your organization fits in the Alignment Matrix. Ask which policies are aligned or misaligned. Define what success would look like if business outcomes improved:

- Revenue and profit increases
- Customer retention
- Employee retention
- Health-related benefit cost reductions

Use these guidelines to develop clear statements about the purpose of realignment and metrics that will be used to measure success.

Step 2: Measure and Monitor *Work* and *Pay*

It is impossible to reward performance unless there is a measure of performance. This is best done with a complete, integrated business database that includes the following information about people:

- All "people" data (who they are, what they do, where they are located)
- Health data (medical and pharmacy utilization)
- Payroll
- Absence data
- Disability claims (short-term and long-term)
- Workers' compensation
- Employee opinions (engagement, satisfaction, etc.)

And information about business outcomes:

- Individual performance
- Business outcomes (operations, production, sales, customer satisfaction, etc)

At the very least, help employees see a direct "line-of-sight" from their job to both revenues and profits. Agree on specific performance results and consider tying those results to variable pay. Keep track of this information in your overall database. Similarly, measuring and tracking both payroll and human resource expenditures, by person, is the only way to monitor compensation and calculate performance indicators such as net diem.

Data management capabilities have advanced in functionality and declined in cost so dramatically, there is virtually no excuse for *not* putting all business information together in one system. Create an online report, a visual dashboard, of essential business metrics you wish to track and monitor them regularly. The report should be a tool used weekly or monthly by a team of leaders for whom it will be meaningful across several areas of the company.

Step 3: Create a Continuous, Transparent Dialog About the Work-for-Pay Exchange

a) Provide a complete accounting of *all* components of pay for every employee on at least an annual basis. This should include all spending by the company on wages, bonuses, training, profit sharing, health benefits, time off, life insurance, dependent care, etc. (see table 11 and fig. 13 on next page).

b) Have regular company or division meetings showing performance, including net diem, revenue, or other key metrics. Allow discussion about what made results better or worse since the last performance review.

c) Translate any changes in pay practices into "what's in it" for all parties.

Step 4: Reallocate and Align Incentives

In ways that improve alignment of both rewards and responsibilities, begin the process of aligning business practices. If both

Table 11: Sample total compensation report

Total Compensation Report 2011 John Q. Employee			
Category	Percent of base	2011 Actual	% of Total
Base Salary		50,000	70%
Variable Pay			
Top Line bonus	4%	$2,000	
Performance bonus	6%	$3,000	
Profit Share	4%	$2,000	
Total	14%	**$7,000**	10%
Benefit Detail			
401K Match (deferred comp)	4%	$2,000	
Statutory Employment Taxes			
FICA	6.02%	$3,100	
Medicare	1.45%	$ 725	
FUTA	0.08%	$ 56	
SUTA	Fixed	$ 127	
Employer Sponsored Benefits			
Health Savings Account		$2,000	
Employer Paid Health Insurance		$3,674	
Training Fees		$1,200	
Value of Paid Time-Off (7 days)		$1,346	
Total		$14,228	20%
All Compensation		**$71,728**	100%

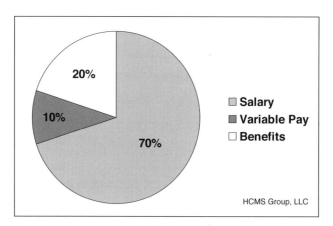

Figure 13: Sample employee total compensation 2010

rewards and responsibilities need realignment, it is important to communicate honestly but with a positive emphasis to employees. For example, if there will be changes to benefit policies, explain that such changes are strategic to improving rewards and training, rather than saying, "Cuts will be made to save money."

Step 5: Build a Platform For an Ownership Mentality

Aligned incentives are built on a philosophy of shared success. You are asking employees to act like owners (and if stock options are available, they may actually be owners). A powerful way to reinforce this attitude is with adoption of a company-wide, quality-improvement process such as Lean Six Sigma.[27] If employees will share rewards for success and share responsibility for problems, it only makes sense to empower them to improve the way work gets done. Another term for this is *decision latitude*. There is good evidence that allowing people to have discretion over how their works gets done lowers stress levels and may translate into confident decision-making in other aspects of life as well.

---

27. George M, Rowland D. Kastle B. *What is Lean Six Sigma?* New York: McGraw-Hill, 2004.

CHAPTER 8

HEALTH PROTECTION AND OTHER SIDE-EFFECTS OF ALIGNMENT

Consider these observations:

- Workers who were eligible for bonuses opted to get a voluntary flu shot at twice the rate of those in the same company not eligible for bonuses.[28]

- Workers who had greater levels of variable pay rated health as more important to their careers.[29]

- Controlling for other factors, higher bonuses are associated with lower rates of smoking and higher rates of compliance with chronic disease medication.[30]

28. Health as Human Capital Foundation.Aligning Incentives: What do bonuses have to do with reducing absence? More than you might think. Entry 2 - 2008. Jan 20, 2008; http://hhcf.blogspot.com/2008/01/aligning-incentives-what-do-bonuses.html (accessed April 27, 2010).
29. Lynch, W., Gardner, H., Melkonian, A., Kleinman, N. Benefits, Rewards and Importance of Health. May 2007; http://www.hhcfoundation.org/hhcf/Publications/Surveys/Brief2.pdf (accessed November 15, 2010).
30. Lynch, W., Gardner, H., Melkonian, A., Kleinman, N. Make it matter, make it possible, make it theirs. White Paper. August 2008; http://www.hhcfoundation.org/hhcf/Publications/WhitePapers/Make%20It%20Rev.pdf (accessed November 15, 2010).

- There is a strong, consistent relationship between higher bonuses and lower rates of disability claims.[31]

Why are these observations true? When workers have strong incentives to be at work and perform well, health is more valuable to them. While this outcome has been surprising to some people who joke that we believe money cures illnesses, it actually makes perfect sense.

Consider the same worker, Bob, in one of two jobs: an aligned Partner culture or a misaligned Entitled culture. In the Partner job, he will earn large rewards for high performance and share expense in the form of reduced pay if absent. In the Entitled job, he has little reward for better performance and shares no expense when using his extensive allowance of time off. Now imagine Bob as he faces health decisions. Should he exercise regularly to maintain a high energy level, or skip that? Should he manage his asthma carefully to make sure he doesn't miss work due to a preventable serious episode?

For each of these decisions, the Partner setting offers more incentive to protect health than the Entitled setting. The Partner employee will potentially lose opportunity, miss out on bonuses and pay more for absence and medical expenses. The Entitled employee loses very little. And if work is unsatisfying, an illness episode may even provide a chance to get away from work for a few days and make the same amount of income.

In our own company, we provide employees with a high-deductible health insurance plan and a HSA funded at $2,000 per

---

31. Health as Human Capital Foundation. Aligning Incentives: What do bonuses have to do with reducing absence? More than you might think. Entry 2 - 2008. Jan 20, 2008; http://hhcf.blogspot.com/2008/01/aligning-incentives-what-do-bonuses.html (accessed April 27, 2010).

year (for individuals, more for families). As you will recall, these are elements of shared responsibilities and shared rewards. One of our younger employees commented that, after five years, she considers her fund, which has now accumulated almost $10,000, to be an additional savings account that she does not want to spend if she doesn't have to. She has a strong, aligned incentive to save money by staying well. She considers her exercise routine to be a direct strategy for saving more money that she can use later in life.

EVIDENCE: SHARED REWARDS AND IMPORTANCE OF HEALTH

This topic has, by far, received the most attention from audiences who hear our presentations, partly because it has been misinterpreted. We have heard people incorrectly paraphrase the connection between bonuses and health this way: "Wendy says that if you throw money at workers, all their diseases will magically disappear." Not exactly.

The message we wanted to deliver was not that money cures diseases, but that traditional work contracts have made health *matter* less to workers. If a worker will be paid the same amount and have no greater out-of-pocket expense whether he is well or ill, staying healthy simply matters less. To make health matter more, compensation and individual responsibility need to be tied more tightly to work performance and use of resources.

When health benefits *and* compensation packages are designed such that employees have something to gain by being productive, and something to lose by not staying healthy, health matters more. This was a profound discovery for me. Rather than telling workers what to do, we need to provide a reason why they should. The usual approach to health has been to ask workers to *please* stop smoking and exercise more. Instead, we should provide meaningful incentives that reward high performance and health protection.

Fewer Rules!

We recently reviewed a sick leave policy that was six pages long. It was very thorough, describing what constituted 'legitimate' illness, how the illness would be verified, how long afterward the worker had to notify the company of a medical absence for it to qualify and many, many more rules. Although the following words were not written on the document, it was clear: "We are worried employees will misuse this policy, so we are trying to anticipate and close every loophole we possibly can."

Of course, some rules are necessary and intuitively designed to keep us from harm, such as: "no running with scissors!" Or "don't ever touch the hot stove!" In other words, some rules protect the young from consequences they cannot fully understand, or protect us from hidden dangers. Other rules are intended to protect others, such as setting speed limits on roads, or setting building requirements for strong structural safety. While some rules make sense, too often we find ourselves spending time and money devising and enforcing rules that are only necessary because we created a poorly-designed system in the first place.

If we require a lot of detailed rules, was the system misaligned to begin with? Whenever you see a long set of rules, it probably means the system has created incentives that remove real-life consequences and accountability from the decision maker. Remember, we all make decisions based on incentives; if we believe a certain action will harm us or those we love, or is not worth the cost, we simply won't do it unless coerced. If a behavior has significant benefit to us and little or no risk or cost involved, it is more likely we will do it.

In the case of the very complex sick-leave policy, the intention seemed to be to protect individuals from a loss of income when they become ill. However, when employees bear no financial accountability for their absence and have no other way to gain value from paid days-off, the misaligned incentive actually encourages people to be absent *when they are not ill*. Naturally, it takes a lot of rules to keep people from misusing time off when the incentives promote just that.

Incentive alignment reduces the need for rules. In the simplest example, pay-for-performance eliminates the need for a large portion of work attendance rules. If my compensation is based on a commission every time I sell your product, or a fee for every task I complete, there is less need for rules about what hours I work, where I work, or how I do my work. In many cases, rules about work hours and work location exist because the employer pays workers for time instead of output.

So, it isn't surprising that there are rules to make sure people complete the necessary hours, when almost no rules would be needed if pay were based on output instead. Strict regulations about how work resources (phones, vehicles, equipment) are used become less necessary if employees bear some accountability for operational costs, or profit. When wasteful spending affects one's own bonus, abuse drops off quickly.

In our company, there are only two rules about time off: 1) let someone know as far in advance as you can and 2) check with others to see that responsibilities get covered. That is because we have no paid-time-off policy. Instead, we are paid the value of paid time-off in each month's salary. Within the limits of getting one's work done, we can then take as much or as little as we want and it is subtracted from pay. This way, each of us takes the time we need, according to our own value for that time. One can hardly "misuse" a benefit you pay for yourself.

As a new father in our company reminded us, this also prevents employees from having to "save up" time when an important event occurs, like a new child arriving in the family. It is the employee's choice to take more time. Under standard PTO policies, the employee may have to choose between a vacation and helping with an important event.

Positive Business Practice Incentives Have Ripple Effects on Many Aspects of Employee Behavior

An aligned absence policy has broader implications than *just* attendance. An aligned pay-for-performance policy changes more than productivity. Our research shows that most business practices extend beyond their particular domain.

Table 12 shows just how connected policies can be. This table reflects general relationships across almost a million employees working for companies with different business practices.

Table 12: Effects of different realignment strategies

Realignment	Effect on the following			
	Productivity	Turnover of Top Performers	Absence Rates	Medical Costs
Increase pay-for performance	Strong improvement	Strong improvement	Improvement	Improvement
Shared absence responsibility	Improvement	None*	Strong improvement	Improvement
Shared medical responsbility	None	None*	Improvement	Strong improvement
Increase training opportunities	Improvement	Improvement	Weak Improvement	None

* Unless rewards are very misaligned.

These synergies are not accidental; they result from a collective current. Showing up, working hard, staying healthy, and gaining skills result in tangible rewards. *Not* showing up, not performing, and not caring for oneself will have negative consequences in terms of money or opportunity.

Alignment multiplies. Getting sick results in missed work. Missing work lowers performance. Lower performance means less bonus pay.

Aligning Manager Behavior: Reducing Workers' Compensation Costs By 65%

Alignment works in other managerial circumstances as well. Remember, the goal is to align the interests of the individual, in this case the manager, with the interests of the company.

Consider an actual example. A large transportation company with a workers' compensation problem had high injury-treatment costs and absence rates, resulting in significant overtime pay expenses. Detailed data revealed an interesting pattern: a small percent of workers had repeat subjective injury claims and then remained absent for four-or five-times as long as the average worker. Further investigation uncovered a reason for the pattern. Managers typically categorized these workers as "problem" cases. It was easier to have them out of sight than manage their performance or terminate them. In other words, incentives were misaligned. Problem workers continued to get paid and their mangers could avoid an unpleasant task without any consequence.

Our team worked with the organization to align incentives. A charge-back system was implemented so that budgets for each manager were to be charged the cost of workers' compensation, medical costs, and absence claims. Manager bonuses were changed to reflect, in part, budget reconciliation and overtime rates. Over a two-year period, overall rates of injury declined only slightly, but repeat short- and long-duration absences became much less frequent.

CHAPTER 9

MISALIGNED CURRENTS HAVEN'T AFFECTED YOU YET? JUST WAIT

When Business Is Good...

O ften business leaders will comment that their currents (incentives) are not strongly aligned but everything is going "just fine." Perhaps, they conclude, misaligned incentives don't matter much.

Actually, like most aspects of life, including family and other relationships, when everyone is happy and stress is low, problems often stay below the surface. Take this example:

A medical products company that later became a client of ours experienced a dramatic growth phase from 2002 to 2007. Wall Street sang its praises, revenues grew exponentially, headcount increased steadily and large bonuses became routine. During that same period, human resources managers reported that medical and absence cost had been kept low and even declined from 2005 through 2007 (see fig. 14) compared to dramatic increases widely experienced elsewhere in those years. This occurred despite a rich benefit plan (the firm falls in the Pampered quadrant) and executives credited their success to investments in superior health improvement and wellness programs.

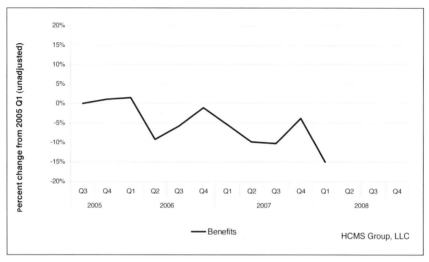

Figure 14: Total benefit costs during corporate growth

But Then...

In early 2008, the company's market share declined rapidly. For the first time in many years, revenues were down, a hiring freeze went into effect and layoffs became a real possibility. It was the company's first serious financial challenge.

Anyone who understands incentive alignment can predict what happened next. Employees had little incentive to use resources carefully and worried about possibly losing them if jobs were eliminated. The result?

Combined healthcare and absence costs increased by 33% in eight months (see fig. 15)! Obviously, company officials who had attributed the flat trend to good health could not simply argue that all employees got sick on March 1, 2008. Instead, the extreme trend was the result of misaligned incentives during a stressful time in the organization.

The lesson this organization learned is that good times may postpone some of the negative consequences of misaligned incentives, but bad times will magnify them. Aligned incentives are even more critical in stressful times, to keep everyone on the same page.

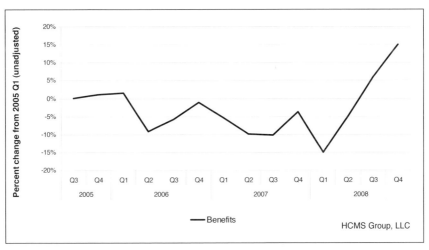

Figure 15: Total benefit costs during corporate decline

On the Other Hand...

At our firm of about 60 employees, we faced a difficult economic climate in 2009 like almost everyone else. Every employee shared the pain, in the form of lower or no performance bonuses, cutbacks in some optional training programs, and delayed replacement of equipment. Despite these lean months, we had almost no turnover, and none of the excessive absences or healthcare spending patterns so often seen during stressful periods at other companies.

Certainly, no one receiving less pay was happy about it. However, the mood was one of a determined team facing business challenges together. We believe that was because employees were given information about what was happening (bad news as well as good news), possible consequences, what our business priorities had to be, and what recovery would look like. Employees had shared rewards during good times and now shared in cutbacks during tough times.

Happily, as revenue improved, employees heard that the top business priority was investing funds into the incentive pool to quickly return to measurable incentive-based pay. Even now, when more job opportunities are available, very few of our employees have chosen to leave.

CHAPTER 10

ONE LAST THOUGHT

Do Aligned Currents Make Everything Perfect? Of Course Not

As we've explained, aligned incentives create a directional pull toward business success, much the way a current in a river acts to draw boats in a certain direction. Even so, currents and business practice incentives do not *force* behavior. Just as some workers may be productive in an Entitlement culture, some may also fail in a system with well-aligned incentives. The current pulls everyone in a specific direction, changing the general culture. It doesn't *make* anyone do anything. Ultimately, incentives cause high performance and low expenses to be more likely. And the stronger, more aligned the currents, the more likely those outcomes become.

If You Hear Nothing Else, Hear This

Aligned incentives can turn around a failing business, jump-start employee careers, make work more satisfying and rewarding, and encourage people to invest in their own health and wellbeing. This is not an exaggeration. We hope the examples we've given and the steps we have outlined help thousands of companies, big and small, align with success.

To summarize, the benefits of aligning your shared rewards and shared responsibilities currents are:

Aligned Incentives Improve Business Success.

Never underestimate the power of collective effort. In some instances misaligned incentives only create small disruptions; an extra absence here, a small amount of wasted time there. But they add up. Collectively, currents either help us succeed together or cause us to drift away from our goals.

Aligned Incentives Improve Efficiency.

It may not be magic, but the effect can certainly be miraculous. When a work contract outlines specifically what a person must do to earn a desired reward, previously scattered efforts become focused on what counts.

Aligned Incentives Reduce Healthcare Costs And Encourage Human Capital Growth.

When workers accept positive and negative consequences for their own performance, they recognize and value their own human capital more. When increased skills or maintaining a healthy lifestyle translates into better opportunities, each of us has a reason to protect, take ownership, and invest in our own health and abilities.

Aligned Incentives Create Constructive Business Partnerships.

Industry needs to evolve. Paternalistic employment arrangements have encouraged an unhealthy dependence and an 'us-versus-them' business culture. Shared success will encourage the type of innovation businesses need.

Aligned Incentives Simplify Work Rules.

As we saw in Chapter 8, many rules are imposed to deter behaviors that misaligned incentives encourage. By aligning employee and company interests, we reduce the number of definitions and rules needed to govern behavior.

All in all, you will never find a more straightforward, understandable way to put everyone on the same team. Stop blaming employees for drifting along in currents that the company created. Start building an environment that pulls everyone toward mutual success.

WHAT'S NEXT? TACKLING HEALTHCARE COSTS WITH ALIGNED INCENTIVES

Aligned incentives and accurate, timely information for doctors and patients—those are the necessary elements to improving quality and managing the cost of healthcare.

The same principles described in this book for improving business performance apply to healthcare. Consumers won't care about price unless they share the cost and can find information. Doctors won't search for equally-effective but less-costly alternatives unless their pay reflects it, or their patients demand it.

In today's system, even *after* reform, both patients and doctors receive greater financial value from their healthcare coverage for being ill than being well. Doctors and hospitals receive more money for providing expensive care, necessary or not, than for providing less-costly, effective treatments. Further, unless they have health savings accounts, consumers must use medical services to get value from their healthcare benefits; healthier workers receive the least value. Worse, a cost-conscious consumer usually cannot find cost or quality information on which to make better decisions. Too often, medical personnel discourage them from asking because "insurance will pay anyway, so don't worry."

The greatest fallacy of healthcare is believing that skyrocketing costs are driven by how sick and old our population has become and that better access to medical care will make cost and quality improve. Actually, high costs reflect misaligned incentives and a lack of information that discourage every person in the system (patient and provider alike) from choosing effective, efficient and prudent alternatives in prevention and treatment. Our system discourages the very types of innovation that could make care affordable, available, and more effective.

Well before the heated debates surrounding passage of healthcare reform in early 2010, business leaders were well aware that costs were out of control. The heavy burden of healthcare costs reduces money available for businesses to invest in other mission-critical resources.

Now that government has passed new rules, the need for aligned incentives is as critical as ever. In our next book, we describe what our research team has learned about effective and ineffective care, about waste and efficiency, about the over-utilization associated with "free" care, and how demonstration projects have documented the power of aligned incentives.

Stay tuned for the next volume.

APPENDIX

Overview of Survey Methods

The survey was administered to a convenience panel of 5,900 potential respondents who are members of the Zoomerang survey panel population (http://www.zoomerang.com). To become eligible as a respondent, panel members have provided personal demographic information and are connected to the internet. Panel members receive gift points for merchandise from the survey company for each survey they complete. The sample population chosen for this survey was chosen from a population of members who recently indicated that they were employed and were distributed across age and gender categories similar to those of the employed U.S. population. The survey was administered via a web application and all responses were received within five days. A total of 1,872 responses were collected, a 32% response rate. Of these, 1,826 respondents were currently employed and included in subsequent analysis.

All items required a forced response, meaning that respondents had to complete all questions to continue. Sometimes "not applicable" was an option. The only exceptions were details regarding bonuses, which were skipped for those not eligible for bonuses. Additionally, for all items featuring longer lists of choices, responses were displayed in a random order to each respondent to minimize effects of order on response patterns.

Responses to several questions were recoded for analysis. For example, salary and bonus categories were assigned a dollar value according to the median number in the reported range. Questions where respondents reported the frequency with which factors affected their productivity were assigned conservative percentage values approximating their response (never=0%, not often=10%, sometimes= 25%, frequently = 50% and always = 100%). Recoding also was used to combine answers to several questions, such as a sum of the total number of different benefits a person reported receiving from their employer.

Characteristics of Respondents

Respondents resembled the employed population of U.S. workers in many respects. Survey respondents were widely distributed in terms of age and almost equally split between male (48%) and female (52%) workers. Compared to the national population of U.S. workers reported by the Bureau of Labor Statistics, the survey respondents had a higher representation of female workers (52% compared to 47%).[32] Among age groups, survey respondents were made up of a higher portion of workers in their twenties and sixties, and a lower portion of workers in their forties than the national workforce.

Respondents were predominantly Caucasian (85%), with only small numbers of other ethnic groups (5% African American, 3%

---

32. Bureau of Labor Statistics. Table 8. Employed and Unemployed Full- and Part-Time Workers by Age, Sex, Race, and Hispanic or Latino Ethnicity: 2009. http://www.bls.gov/cps/cpsaat8.pdf (accessed Nov 16, 2010).

Latino/Hispanic, 3% Asian). Less than one percent of respondents had not completed high school. Asked about the highest level of education, respondents reported 14% with a high school degree, 36% with some college, 32% completing a bachelors degree, and the remaining 17% having a masters degree or higher. These levels of higher education are more advanced than the general U.S. population, where 30% have a high school education, 18% have some college, 16% have a bachelors degree and only 8% have a masters degree or higher.[33] Employed workers usually held full-time positions with a company. However, 11% were self-employed and just over 2% were employed part time.

33. U.S. Census Bureau. Table 1. Educational Attainment of the Population 18 Years and Over, by Age, Sex, Race and Hispanic Origin: 2009. http://www.census.gov/hhes/socdemo/education/ (accessed Nov 16, 2010).

GLOSSARY

Absenteeism: The rate at which employees miss work. This usually refers to days absent from work for which the employee is being paid (or paid time-off).

Alignment: In the context of this book, alignment refers to a shared interest in the same goals or outcomes. Specifically, 'incentive alignment' is the degree to which monetary or other intangible incentives and rewards encourage all parties to behave in ways that that are mutually beneficial.

Benefits, or fringe benefits: Benefits encompass all forms of compensation that a company provides for employees in addition to wages. Common types of benefits include paid holidays and sick leave, retirement or 401K matching, and health insurance. In some cases benefits include services such as fitness center memberships or child care.

Bonus or performance bonus: By most definitions, bonuses include any additional earnings given to employees outside of regular salary. Performance bonuses, by contrast, are additional earnings awarded to employees that are linked to either individual or company performance. For example, a bonus given to every employee, regardless of the company's relative performance, is not a performance bonus; it simply functions as additional salary. Performance bonuses are also referred to a variable pay, meaning they increase or decrease to reflect performance.

Cash-out leave: Also called cash-back leave, this refers to a company policy that allows employees to exchange their unused sick leave for additional pay. In some cases, the money is only awarded when the employee leaves his job. In other cases, employees can choose to cash out a portion of unused time off at designated intervals (e.g., annually). Cash-out policies are an alternative to use-it-or-lose-it policies that require employees to be absent or forfeit unused days.

CDHP: Consumer-directed health plan. This form of health-related benefits refers to the combination of a high-deductible health plan (the details of which must meet federal requirements) and a health account. Health accounts can be either a Health Savings Account, the balance of which an employee can take with him when he changes jobs, or a Health Reimbursement Arrangement, the balance of which an employee must forfeit when leaving a job.

Compensation: All of the financial and non-financial payments and services an employee receives in exchange for work; also referred to as Total Rewards. In some cases, the terms *compensation* and *benefits* are used separately to distinguish between pay and other services. However, in this book, compensation refers to the sum of all financial and non-financial payments.

Currents: A metaphor for the direction in which a company's policies and/or incentives are pulling employees. If a company's incentives are aligned with company success, its policies and rewards will create "currents" that pull employees toward lower benefit costs and higher productivity. If incentives are misaligned, the company's underlying currents will pull employees toward higher benefit costs and lower productivity.

Deferred compensation: Pay that is awarded in a form for which the employee will become eligible to receive at a later date. The most common forms of deferred compensation are matched funds in 401K accounts (or their equivalent), and pension or retirement plans.

Disease: Any diagnosed illness. In most cases when we refer to a person having a disease or a number if diseases, those are defined as diagnoses recorded in healthcare claims data.

Disengaged: In our shared-reward and shared-responsibility matrix, the Disengaged quadrant refers to workforces that have little reward for hard work, but are asked to take accountability for protecting resources. These employees have low rewards and high responsibility.

Entitled: A sense that one deserves to receive certain services or payments. It usually refers to circumstances where there is debate whether the person has earned the services to which they feel entitled. In our shared-reward and shared-responsibility matrix, the Entitled quadrant refers to workforces where there are few rewards for hard work, and little accountability for protecting resources. These employees have low rewards and low responsibility.

ERISA: The Employee Retirement Income Security Act, enacted in 1974. ERISA usually refers to an entire suite of laws regulating employee benefits, requirements about communication of those benefits, minimum standards about many types of benefits, and legal protection of employee rights.

HDHP: High-deductible health plan. Although there is no single definition, plans with a deductible of $1,500 or more for an individual are often referred to as such.

Health savings account (HSA): An account that allows individuals or their employer to deposit pre-tax money for the purposes of covering medical expenses. Account holders must have a qualifying HDHP and are limited on the amount deposited each year, both of which are defined annually by the IRS. Funds in the account can be used with no tax penalty for medical expenses until age 65, after which the funds can be used for any purpose. An HSA is owned by the employee and is portable between jobs.

Human Capital: The inherent capacity each individual possesses to contribute to his family, work, or community. In our definition, this consists of three assets: skills, motivation, and health. Depending on investment in and growth of each asset, each person may or may not reach his or her full human capital capacity.

Incentive: Any possible anticipated outcome a person finds desirable. Incentives can come in the form of verbal praise, public recognition, money, opportunities for training or other services, or items of perceived value. Similarly, a disincentive is any possible outcome a person finds undesirable and works to avoid.

Income replacement rate: This refers to the portion of salary that a person receives from a disability insurance policy (STD or LTD) while absent from work due to illness.

Lean Six Sigma: A widely-used quality improvement approach that is used by businesses to evaluate and improve inefficiencies in manufacturing or providing services. It is a variation on Six

Sigma, an approach trademarked by Motorola that focuses on minimizing defects (error rates, or problems). It involves an ongoing process of systematic inquiry about how operations can be improved. When adopted across a company, every employee at every level becomes a valuable contributor to the continuous-improvement process.

Long-term disability (LTD): A form of insurance that pays a portion (usually between 60 and 70%) of an employee's salary in the event that a medical condition prevents him from working for a longer period. Usually, LTD begins six months after an employee has been absent from work.

Moral hazard: An economic term that refers to the known tendency for individuals to behave differently when someone else takes responsibility for potential consequences. The two most common examples are that 1) individuals will consume more of a good or service when someone else pays for that good or service, and 2) individuals will take more risk if someone else will bear the consequences if something goes wrong (e.g., insurance).

OSHA: This acronym refers to either the Occupational Safety and Health Administration, a federal agency of the United States that regulates workplace safety and health, or the Occupational Safety and Health Act, a federal law created in 1970 to improve safety and reduce known hazards in workplaces. The Administration oversees rules about workplace safety and collects data about accidents and injuries.

Out-of-pocket: The portion of costs that the individual pays for healthcare services.

Paid time-off (PTO): Various types of allowed days for which employees can receive pay despite not working. The most common forms of paid time off are holidays, sick leave, vacation, short-term disability and long-term disability. The abbreviation PTO can also refer to a PTO "bank" where most forms of paid time-off (vacation, holiday, sick leave) are combined into one single number of days rather than keeping them split apart.

Pampered: In our shared-reward and shared-responsibility matrix, the Pampered quadrant refers to workforces where there are significant rewards for hard work, but no accountability for protecting resources. These employees have high rewards and low responsibility.

Partner: In our shared-reward and shared-responsibility matrix, the Partner quadrant refers to workforces that have fully aligned policies and incentives. These workforces have significant rewards for hard work, and are asked to take accountability for protecting resources. These employees have high rewards and high responsibility.

Pay: The exchange made on the part of an employer in return for an employee's work.

Pay-for-performance: Another term referring to bonuses awarded in return for individual or team performance.

Performance metric or measurement: Specific ways of tracking how productive or successful an employee or group of employees are.

Productivity: The level of output or accomplishment of an employee or group of employees.

Profit sharing: A form of variable pay where employees receive bonuses that reflect how profitable the company was during a specified time period.

Quality Improvement Programs: Systematic processes used by organizations to reduce errors or defects and improve efficiency and quality. Examples of Quality improvement programs include Six Sigma and Lean Six Sigma. The evolution of these processes are most often credited to W. Edwards Deming who helped streamline manufacturing in Japanese companies in the 1940s and 50s.

Rewards: See shared rewards.

Salary: Regular pay, usually predefined and only changes annually or when responsibilities change.

Shared Responsibilities: The extent to which company policies and benefits are designed in ways that ask employees to share accountability for the resources they spend. This can be in the form of a high deductible or coinsurance on health insurance plans, or receiving a lower portion of pay during disability, or asking for their participation in quality improvement efforts. A list of shared responsibilities is shown in Chapter 3.

Shared Rewards: The extent to which employees experience personal gains when they perform well or stay healthy. This can include performance bonuses, deposits in a health savings account, or investments in training. A list of shared rewards is shown in Chapter 3.

Short-term disability (STD): A form of insurance that pays a portion (usually between 60 and 100%) of an employee's salary in the event that a medical condition prevents him from working for an extended period of time. Short-term disability commonly is longer than two weeks, but less than six months.

Use-it-or-lose-it benefits: Any rule that requires benefits such as vacation, sick-leave, or flexible spending accounts be consumed within a designated time period or forfeited.

Variable pay: The same as a performance bonus. Variable pay is additional earnings awarded to employees that are linked to either individual or company performance. When performance is better, pay is higher. When performance is lower, pay is lower.

Wages: Regular monetary pay. It can be either in the form of salary (predefined) or hourly.

Work: The efforts made by an employee in exchange for pay.

INDEX

misaligned incentives, 20, 30,
    65, 74, 77, 107, 109, 112–113,
    116
CDHP (consumer-directed health
    plan), see health plan design
compensation, x, xiv, 13, 19, 25,
    43, 65, 71, 73–74, 83, 92, 94–
    95, 101, 103, 105, 121–123
compensation report, 96
consumer-directed health plan
    (CDHP), see health plan
    design
cost drivers, see causes of
    healthcare utilization
costs, see benefits; healthcare
    costs; modifiable costs
currents, 64, 66, 72, 79, 93, 111–
    113, 122–123
    a metaphor for incentives, 35–59
    misaligned, 107–110

D

data, x–xi, 2–3, 19, 41, 45–51, 69,
    72–74, 94–95, 105, 123, 125
decision latitude, 97
decision making, 54
deductibles, see health plan design
deferred compensation, 123
Deming, W. Edwards, 127
demographics
    education, xiii, 31, 75, 119
    gender, xii, 15, 48, 52, 55, 74,
    76, 117
diem, see net diem
disadvantages, of more benefits, 18
disease, 3, 8, 78, 99, 101, 123

"Disengaged" Quadrant, 64–65,
    91, 123

E

economic principles, 2, 4
education, xiii, 31, 75, 119
eligibility for bonuses, see
    performance bonuses
employee compensation report, 96
Employee Retirement Income
    Security Act (1974) (ERISA),
    17, 123
employer-based health insurance,
    16
employment agreements, see work
    contracts
"Entitled" Quadrant, 65–65, 100,
    123
ERISA, see Employee Retirement
    Income Security Act (1974)
evidence, x, xiv
    bonuses, 15
    defining shared rewards, 47–48
    disadvantages of more benefits,
    18
    how we know what we know, x–
    xiv
    matrix, motivation and resource
    use, 68–69
    measuring value, 91–92
    rewards in general, 15–16
    shared responsibilities, 54–56
    shared rewards and the
    importance of health, 101–102
    using benefits because you have
    them, 22–23